Modern TypeScript

A Practical Guide to Accelerate
Your Development Velocity

Ben Beattie-Hood

Apress®

Modern TypeScript: A Practical Guide to Accelerate Your Development Velocity

Ben Beattie-Hood
Melbourne, VIC, Australia

ISBN-13 (pbk): 978-1-4842-9722-3
https://doi.org/10.1007/978-1-4842-9723-0

ISBN-13 (electronic): 978-1-4842-9723-0

Managing Director, Apress Media LLC: Welmoed Spahr
Acquisitions Editor: James Robinson-Prior
Development Editor: James Markham
Editorial Assistant: Gryffin Winkler

Cover designed by eStudioCalamar

Distributed to the book trade worldwide by Springer Science+Business Media New York, 1 New York Plaza, Suite 4600, New York, NY 10004-1562, USA. Phone 1-800-SPRINGER, fax (201) 348-4505, e-mail orders-ny@springer-sbm.com, or visit www.springeronline.com. Apress Media, LLC is a California LLC and the sole member (owner) is Springer Science + Business Media Finance Inc (SSBM Finance Inc). SSBM Finance Inc is a **Delaware** corporation.

For information on translations, please e-mail booktranslations@springernature.com; for reprint, paperback, or audio rights, please e-mail bookpermissions@springernature.com.

Apress titles may be purchased in bulk for academic, corporate, or promotional use. eBook versions and licenses are also available for most titles. For more information, reference our Print and eBook Bulk Sales web page at http://www.apress.com/bulk-sales.

Any source code or other supplementary material referenced by the author in this book is available to readers on GitHub. For more detailed information, please visit https://www.apress.com/gp/services/source-code.

Paper in this product is recyclable

Table of Contents

About the Author

Ben Beattie-Hood is a principal software engineer and professional mentor with over 20 years of industry experience. He currently specializes in front-end technology, technical strategy, system design, and development and training in TypeScript, React, and related technologies.

Ben is passionate about evolvable systems, about creating learning organizations, and about how ideas are formed and communicated. He has given a wide range of talks covering product development, event sourcing microservices, event storming practice, modern database internals, functional programming, front-end design and build, as well as coaching in TypeScript as a velocity tool.

Ben lives with his beautiful wife and two children in Melbourne, Australia, where he loves to hike and travel.

About the Technical Reviewer

 **Oscar Velandia** is a front-end developer at
Stahls. He has worked the past four years
with Typescript, transitioning projects from
Vanilla JavaScript to TypeScript, creating MVP
projects, and working on large TypeScript,
Next.js, and React code bases.

CHAPTER 1

How TypeScript Came to Be

Introduction

As we start our TypeScript journey, we delve into the background of this powerful programming language. To truly grasp the capabilities of TypeScript, it is essential to understand its roots and the context in which it evolved. We'll take a brief trip through the history of JavaScript and ECMAScript and how these played into the development of TypeScript in late 2012. This brief background will help us get both a clearer sense of the problems TypeScript solves as well as the reasoning behind some of the evolution of TypeScript itself. Understanding these key points, around the need for more scalable velocity, and how testing and docs can be delivered in the simplest possible way to solve this will give us a strong foundation for fully understanding the direction and outcomes of the TypeScript language.

History

To truly understand TypeScript, it is important to understand some of the background of the language. We want to get onto the fun stuff with types, but this background is necessary, so I'll keep it short and to the point.

B. Beattie-Hood, *Modern TypeScript*, https://doi.org/10.1007/978-1-4842-9723-0_1

Because when looking into TypeScript, you'll undoubtedly come across references to both JavaScript and ECMAScript and their versions – so how do all these fit together? So let's rewind the clock to get a quick overview.

The first version of JavaScript was released in 1995, and it quickly gained popularity among web developers. In 1996, Microsoft introduced their own version of JavaScript called JScript. And so in 1997, JavaScript was submitted to the European Computer Manufacturers Association (ECMA) in an effort to standardize. This resulting standard was called ECMAScript and was released in 1999.

So the important thing to note here is that ECMAScript is a standard, not a language. That means that it defines *how* features like objects, functions, variables, closures, operators, error handling, etc., *all work and interoperate*, but it doesn't define the actual implementation for them. JavaScript then became the first *implementation* of ECMAScript, defining the syntax and being implemented in runtimes in early browsers.

So ECMAScript v1 (also known as ES1) was released in 1997 and was implemented by concurrent versions of JavaScript. And like any new specification, features missing from the ECMAScript specification quickly began to be found, and so ECMAScript v2 (ES2) was released shortly after in 1998 and ECMAScript v3 (ES3) in 1999.

At this point, the specification allowed for single language files to import values into a global memory space, but things were pretty rudimentary. The next phase of work would be to define how modules worked – how large parcels of code could interoperate without using a global variable store. However, with contention between primary contributors such as Adobe and Mozilla Foundation, eventually the next iteration (ES4) was postponed as a leap that was too great at the time. And without tooling like modules to manage complexity, most projects stabilized on a single or few, manually crafted, monolithic js-file approach, and the industry eventually settled onto using frameworks like jQuery (2006) to facilitate basic-to-midscale UI interactions.

Then in 2008–2009, a series of major breakthroughs occurred in nearly domino effect, which changed the course of the JavaScript, and ECMAScript, ecosystem massively (Figure 1-1).

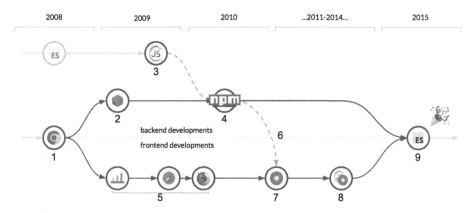

Figure 1-1. *Sequence of major breakthroughs in the JS ecosystem*

1. In 2008, Google released the Chrome browser, with a new, faster JavaScript runtime engine called V8.

2. In 2009, Chrome's new V8 engine was picked up by a team led by Ryan Dahl as the basis for a new server runtime they called Node.js. This ran plain JavaScript, but from a CLI or system service, to support non-front-end tasks.

3. Meanwhile, an independent team of volunteers had been working on an alternative to the stalled ECMAScript module problem – a new JavaScript module workaround they called CommonJS.

4. As Node.js rapidly grew, they needed a way to solve ECMAScript's missing modules problem and so picked up the CommonJS as a suitable workaround. This allowed them to then create the Node Package Manager (NPM) in 2010, as a way of sharing Node.js modules.

5. During all this time, V8's significant increase
    in browser performance triggered further
    improvements in browsers such as Safari and
    Firefox and therefore product potential. This
    renewed interest in JavaScript as a platform for
    delivering user experiences.

6. Larger, more sophisticated user experiences in
    front end were needed, and so the community
    began using NPM as a way of sharing front-end
    packages too.

7. This triggered a new front-end module system
    called Asynchronous Module Definition (a.k.a.
    AMD, via RequireJS), and with this standard, a new
    wave of front-end development began to increase
    with exponential rapidity.

8. To allow module systems to work on both the
    browser *and* on Node.js, a third module system
    grandiosely titled Universal Module Definition was
    released, which basically packaged both AMD and
    CommonJS formats in a single bundle.

9. The renewed development, as well as increasing
    sharding of front- and back-end module systems,
    coupled with the hugely increased contribution and
    investment in the JavaScript ecosystem, saw the
    reconvening of the ECMAScript group and eventual
    creation of the ECMAScript module system (ES
    Modules, or ESM) in 2015.

💡 We explore these module formats in more detail in the "Modules" section in Chapter 8.

Phew – that's a lot to take in! But the main thing you need to know is that during 2009–2010, there was a huge upsurge in the JavaScript ecosystem. This continued to have exponential growth, until NPM became the largest and most active package repository in the world and still continues as such today, 2× larger than *all other public package ecosystems combined* and with now over 32k packages published or updated every month (Figure 1-2).

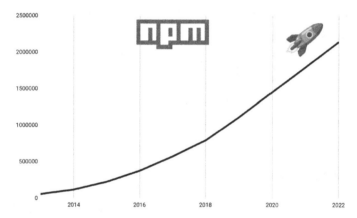

Figure 1-2. *Total number of packages on NPM over recent years*

The Problem

It would be right to say that the JavaScript ecosystem, to put it mildly, is flourishing. To keep up with the rapid development, NPM packages often depend on each other – each package providing specialism in discrete areas, with best-of-breed packages ever emerging. In one recent study, it was found that over 60% of packages had a dependency chain greater than three layers deep; and another found that over 61% of packages could be considered abandoned with dependent ecosystems likely to need to swap them for replacements.

So it comes with the territory in JavaScript that one will be managing dependencies, constantly working out what packages are compatible with others, and trying to test against flaws. But if we have to face continually updating packages, how will we know that an update will still work?

Scalable Velocity

Scalable velocity is important in software development because it enables teams to maintain a consistent pace of development and predictable expectations, even as the project grows in complexity and size. But with an ever-shifting foundation, businesses faced needing to mitigate the risk of continual unknown compatibility.

Fortunately, there are two tools built for ensuring scalable velocity: **Testing** and **Docs**.

Testing Allows Scale

The first tool to protect against churn from ecosystem velocity is exhaustive testing. Ignoring for a moment the problems that overtesting can cause (calcification and friction; we'll come back to these), there's no denying that we can feel confident updating a whole batch of packages if we have tests that ensure our program still works afterward.

And so 2010–2011 saw the rapid increase of JavaScript testing frameworks, such as Jasmine and Mocha. These provided a standardized way to write tests against JavaScript products and as such a way to ensure teams to retain velocity at scale.

But tests are a double-edged sword – they can help certainty and thereby speed development; but exhaustive testing can slow development where tests need large-scale review and updating after changes, and often unit and E2E tests replicate product code and cause changes to effectively need to be written twice.

Docs Allow Scale

Another aspect of maintaining scalable velocity is the need to educate consumers on the changes and how to best use the updated systems. Documentation therefore is our second tool in mitigating difficulty onboarding new versions of packages, by supplying training and deeper understanding for consuming devs.

And so, likewise, 2010–2011 saw the rise of generative or simplified tooling like Dox and the much increased adoption of existing systems like JSDoc.

But writing documentation takes time, and documentation is out of date as soon as you update a product. Reading documentation also takes time and can be hard to convince consumers to do. So returns on documentation can be limited.

Types Provide Both Testing and Docs

So we have two solutions, both imperfect. But if we combine them, can we get something more ideal?

Static testing is the practice of evaluating code without running it. Types perform compatibility checking within your code and between packages and so provide the simplest form of static testing; and types can work as documentation, inlined into dev IDEs and guaranteed to be up to date.

And therefore in October 2012, Microsoft released TypeScript, an at-build-time tool for static testing JavaScript. TypeScript was an implementation of ECMAScript, which surfaced the underlying dynamically asserted types of JavaScript. Using TypeScript, developers didn't have to work out the types of variables and functions in order to understand the code, but instead their IDEs could refer to TypeScript's inline type lints, allowing structural types to be defined explicitly in the code. Running TypeScript checked the contracts for the developer, both providing live compatibility tests (also known as type checks) as well as inline documentation for the structures. This was the best of both solutions in action.

Since then, nearly all large-scale projects have migrated onto TypeScript as a tool for providing documentation and static testing at scale with low friction. Teams using the language have found it much easier, and more reliable, to stay abreast of constant changes in dependencies, and the JavaScript ecosystem has grown faster and even more successfully than before.

Summary

In this chapter, we explored the history of JavaScript and ECMAScript and how these gave birth to a need for scalable velocity and how this was then addressed through types in TypeScript. We saw how TypeScript's ability to perform compatibility checking and provide inline type lints offered the best of both worlds, allowing teams to manage dependencies more confidently and efficiently. And we saw how, as a result, TypeScript adoption skyrocketed, with large-scale projects flocking to leverage its benefits for documentation and static testing.

The stage now set, we are now primed with a better appreciation of the language to delve deeper into TypeScript's core features and dive into the world of structural and computed typing. By harnessing TypeScript's power, you will be able to tackle complex projects, and lean into JavaScript's thriving ecosystem, with complete confidence.

CHAPTER 2

Getting Started with the Developer Experience

Introduction

In this chapter, we will set up your TypeScript development environment and explore the essential tools and configurations needed to streamline your TypeScript projects. A well-configured development environment is crucial for maintaining scalable velocity and effectively managing dependencies.

You will learn how to set up TypeScript from scratch with a no-frills approach, allowing you to run TypeScript files directly from the command line. We'll walk through the process of creating a simple TypeScript file, execute it using the ts-node package, and then leverage Visual Studio Code's debugging capabilities to pause execution and inspect your code during runtime.

We'll then explore a more realistic setup for TypeScript projects, one that leverages best-of-breed packages from the JavaScript ecosystem. We'll introduce you to powerful build and management tools like NX, which

© Ben Beattie-Hood 2023
B. Beattie-Hood, *Modern TypeScript*, https://doi.org/10.1007/978-1-4842-9723-0_2

automate the configuration process, keeping your projects up to date with industry best practices. These tools will empower you to focus on building your applications without worrying about tedious configuration tasks.

By the end of this chapter, you will have a solid understanding of how to set up a TypeScript project for any enterprise need, to build robust and maintainable applications.

Environment and IDE

Currently, most TypeScript and JavaScript builds are done using Node.js, so we'll use that here. To install it, visit `https://nodejs.org/en/download`, and choose the correct version for your operating system.

And for this book, I'll assume you will be using Visual Studio Code. This small, extensible IDE is the de facto standard for most web development and comes with built-in support for TypeScript. It too is simple to install – just visit `https://code.visualstudio.com/download`, and again choose the correct version for your operating system.

No-Frills TypeScript Setup

To get started with a vanilla, zero additions, no-frills setup of TypeScript, create a new folder, open a terminal or command-line there (I'll refer to this as a terminal from now on), and enter the following:

Listing 2-1. A vanilla, no-frills setup of TypeScript

```
npm install typescript ts-node
```

This will create a package.json and package-lock.json for you, and install both TypeScript and ts-node (a package that allows you to run TypeScript directly from Node.js). Now, let's try it out.

Create a folder called "src", and create a file called main.ts within it. Add the following code to the file:

Listing 2-2. /src/main.ts

```
console.log('Hello world!');
```

Now, back in your terminal, type the following and press enter:

Listing 2-3. Running TypeScript from the terminal

```
npx ts-node src/main.ts
```

Congratulations, you've just run your first TypeScript file from the command line!

Debugging TypeScript

Running TypeScript as shown in the preceding examples is fine, but you'll also need to be able to debug TypeScript in order to build at scale. Visual Studio Code comes with support for this, so let's set this up now.

In Visual Studio Code, navigate to debug panel (1); press the "create a launch.json file" link (2) (Figure 2-1).

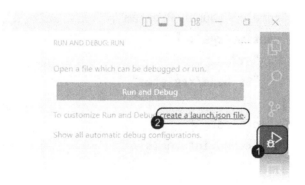

Figure 2-1. *Creating a launch.json file*

Choose "Node.js" (3) from the pop-up list of debugger options (Figure 2-2).

Figure 2-2. *Selecting Node.js as a debugger*

And lastly edit the automatically created "launch.json" file to include the "runtimeArgs" details as follows:

Listing 2-4. Visual Code launch.json

```
{
    "version": "0.2.0",
    "configurations": [
        {
            "type": "node",
            "request": "launch",
            "name": "Launch Program",
            "runtimeArgs": [
                "-r",
                "ts-node/register"
            ],
            "skipFiles": [
                "<node_internals>/**"
            ],
```

```
      "program": "${file}"
   }
 ]
}
```

That's it! Now navigate to a line in your main.ts file that you'd like execution to pause on, and press the F9 key on your keyboard, or click in the left gutter, to create a breakpoint. Now, press the F5 key on your keyboard to run your program, and you'll see the IDE pause on your breakpointed line.

If you want a quick scratch pad for trying out TypeScript code outside your project, you might want to check out the "Quokka.js" extension for Visual Studio Code. This extension will allow you to run TypeScript files live as well as set up live tests against them. It's an easy way to explore the language more, and I've found it an invaluable tool. The free online "TypeScript Playground" (`www.typescriptlang.org/play`) is another similar resource.

Another useful extension to try in Visual Studio Code, while getting into TypeScript, is "Pretty TypeScript Errors." This extension will provide a more readable breakdown of error messages, as well as links to further information and sometimes a video on how to solve them.

Looking good! We can build, run, and debug. And we could go further on this, as there are a lot more options we can pass to TypeScript via config to use it more effectively. We'll get into these later (see Build ➤ Compiler Options); but rather than digging deeper and deeper into those now, let's just pause for a minute and take a reality check.

TypeScript Within a More Realistic Setup

Although you can build and run TypeScript files directly via the CLI as shown previously, TypeScript is honestly better used as part of a larger toolchain – leveraging best-of-breed packages from the JavaScript ecosystem to build large scalable websites, back ends, or native apps. Most books will suggest you clone a custom repo created by the author, pre-set for these configurations; but to be frank, that's not how I'd expect you to use TypeScript in industry. Instead, let's now set up TypeScript as part of a toolchain in the best possible way that will be easy to keep up to date.

Sounds good? But with the JavaScript ecosystem moving so quickly, how are we to keep continually up to date on all the "best practice" configurations and NPM packages for our particular use cases?

Thankfully, the ecosystem has matured to a state where this can be done for you by a couple of useful build and management tools – you no longer need to retain a full-time job learning about build caching, module bundle splitting, and the like – these can take care of these tasks for you.

The first of these is NX. Let's try it out now. Create a new folder, open a terminal there, and enter the following:

Listing 2-5. Installing NX

```
npm install --save-dev @nrwl/next
```

See how we didn't need to install TypeScript or ts-node, or configure either of these to "best practice"? Now, let's use NX to configure our TypeScript project to build a web app, built on Next.js using React and TypeScript:

Listing 2-6. Creating a Next.js+TypeScript+React site using one of NX's built-in templates

```
npx nx g @nrwl/next:app my-new-app
```

Now, without having to configure or maintain it, we have a fully working repo for Next.js using React and TypeScript, with additional build and test tooling out of the box, ready to go. And on top of that, we also don't have to maintain our repo configuration as tooling packages, configurations, and practices come and go out of date.

Honorable Mentions

NX and Turborepo provide a solid basis for frictionless, enterprise-scale development. If you're interested in pushing the boundaries a bit further, some other current tooling worth being aware of at present with TypeScript is listed as follows, for further research:

- Turborepo (`https://turbo.build/`): An alternative to NX, developed by Vercel – the company behind Next.js, a leading React framework and contributor to the React core libraries. It's a little more bare-bones than NX currently, but if you're targeting Next.js/React, it is a more canonical tooling with many useful features.

- ESLint (`https://eslint.org/`, `https://typescript-eslint.io/`): Although TypeScript will check most of your types, there are still rules developed by the community that can assist further for type safety. We'll cover this tool in more detail in the "Linting" section in Chapter 8, later in this book.

- Bun (`https://bun.sh/`): A highly optimized alternative to Node.js, Deno, and others, which includes built-in support for TypeScript with no compilation required.

- Civet (`https://civet.dev/`): A meta-language built on top of TypeScript that provides many functional concepts not yet accepted by the W3C or the TC39 steering committee, such as pattern matching, pipelines, infix operators, chained comparisons, returning conditionals, and much more.

- RedwoodJS (`https://redwoodjs.com/`): A batteries-included alternative to Next.js and others that integrates best-of-breed for each front-end tooling category and provides some simple meta-language that reduces client-server boilerplate.

Summary

In this chapter, we learned how to get started with TypeScript, including how to set up a simple project and how to use a templating tool for more advanced use cases.

We covered the basics of TypeScript, such as installing the **tsc** CLI tool, creating a configuration file, and compiling and debugging TypeScript code. Running and debugging TypeScript files from the terminal and Visual Studio Code allowed us to gain confidence in executing TypeScript code efficiently.

We also explored more advanced use cases by using the templating tool **NX** to generate your TypeScript configuration and allow easy running and debugging of your app. These tools automated the configuration process, sparing us from the need to retain a full-time job learning about various build tasks and module bundling. By leveraging these tools, we created a fully functional Next.js web app, powered by React and TypeScript, without any manual configuration.

To enhance our development experience, we explored useful extensions like "Quokka.js" and "Pretty TypeScript Errors," which provided us with live TypeScript code execution, better error messages, and improved code readability. We also reviewed some additional tools that reduce errors and/or speed development, in ESLint, Bun, Civet, and RedwoodJS.

As we move forward in this book, armed with a well-configured development environment, we'll dive deeper into TypeScript's core concepts and advanced features. By mastering the tools and setup presented in this chapter, you have a solid springboard for successful TypeScript development, building scalable and maintainable applications within the JavaScript ecosystem.

CHAPTER 3

TypeScript Basics

Introduction

In this chapter, we will explore the basics of TypeScript's structural typing system, often known as "duck typing," and how it differs from the hierarchical types offered by traditional object-oriented programming.

Structural typing asserts that the shape or structure of an object is more critical than its instance type or class. JavaScript uses runtime structural typing, and TypeScript supports these structural types by allowing the developer to specify them as contracts pre-build via explicit lint annotations. TypeScript then uses these annotations to check that the inferable type of a value matches the developer's expectations.

In this chapter, we will explore the ways we can use TypeScript to define these "minimum contract" types for values and how structural typing allows various objects to fulfill that contract in a more maintainable and scalable way than traditional inheritance and polymorphism.

We will also explore the concepts of type inference, narrowing and widening, and the interpretation of types via an inbuilt mechanism called "control-flow analysis." We will look at optionality, what to do when you have unknown types, and then begin a deeper dive into more advanced concepts such as simple value vs. parameterized types.

© Ben Beattie-Hood 2023
B. Beattie-Hood, *Modern TypeScript*, https://doi.org/10.1007/978-1-4842-9723-0_3

By the end of this chapter, you will have a deep understanding of structural typing and its applications in TypeScript. You will be equipped with the knowledge and tools to ensure type safety, harnessing the power of TypeScript while embracing the dynamic nature of JavaScript.

Structural Typing

Dynamic languages such as JavaScript use a concept called "structural typing." This is more commonly called "duck typing." Figure 3-1 shows the usual obtuse and confusing picture people will often point you toward when you ask "why is it called duck typing?"

Figure 3-1. *Is this a rabbit or a duck?*

Not very helpful, I agree. But the preceding image actually looks like a duck *and* a rabbit (depending on what you're looking for) – so the point here is that it's somewhat *both* things at the same time, like Schrödinger's cat, being both alive and dead simultaneously. And the analogy goes that you'll only really be able to determine if it's one or the other type if someone adds additional detail, like legs or nose.

What the duck-or-rabbit analogy, or "duck typing" nickname, is getting at is that the **type** or the **class** of an object is *less* important than the **methods it defines**.

I find an easier way to visualize it as shown in Figure 3-2.

Figure 3-2. *The shape of the hole defines the contract*

In the preceding image, whatever is round can fit into the hole. It doesn't matter if it's

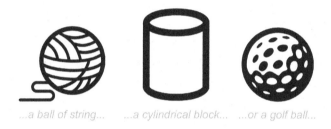

...a ball of string...   ...a cylindrical block...   ...or a golf ball...

If it fits the "contract" delineated by the round hole, it can successfully fit in the round hole (Figure 3-3).

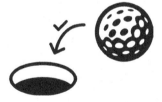

Figure 3-3. *Other items that match the same shape are accepted too*

So that's the way you can think of structural types: **structural types define a minimum shape (or structure) of a value**. And it doesn't matter what the value is, what it inherits from, or anything else really – if it fits the required minimum contract, it's accepted. And while this may seem overly simplistic, in practice, it turns out to be much more powerful, and scalable, than alternative approaches.

This power can take some getting used to, if you come from an object-oriented programming background and are more familiar with using inheritance and polymorphism. So let's illustrate the power of this with a different example, this time with code. Take the following types:

Listing 3-1. Limits of polymorphism, 1

```
interface Toy {            interface Food {   interface Painting {
    manufacturer: string      height: number      height: number
    height: number            width: number       width: number
    width: number             expiry: date        style: string
}                          }                  }
```

Let's say we wanted to put all those things into a cardboard box and wanted to know if they'd all fit. If we were using polymorphism, we'd have to inherit them all from some sort of "ThingWithASize" base class and then define the function like this:

Listing 3-2. Limits of polymorphism, 2

```
class Toy extends ThingWithASizeAbstractType { ... }
class Chair extends ThingWithASizeAbstractType { ... }
class Painting extends ThingWithASizeAbstractType { ... }
```

```
function addToBoxPolymorphically(thing:
ThingWithASizeAbstractType) {
  // ...
}
```

Yuck. And we start to hit problems here, finding that polymorphism isn't really helping us, because in another context (say, storing Purchasables, or Favorites), we can see that those three things *don't* really inherit from a common class – what they inherit from really depends on the context.

A polymorphic approach leads into having strange object taxonomies, trying to force various conflicting contexts and needs into a single polymorphic inheritance tree. Polymorphism also requires that the abstract class inherited is already defined; so any later extension can often require a rewrite, or to try to predict all eventualities in your inheritance tree.

Saleable   Favorite   PhysicalItem

Figure 3-4. *Polymorphism problem: Which base class should we inherit the items from?*

To avoid this problem of inheritance, structural typing proposes instead, "hey, if whatever you're assigning to this value fits this minimum contract, then we're all good" – thereby removing the need for weird arbitrary taxonomies of conflicting contexts.

Making types only a "minimum contract" for what is required by any given context, structural typing also allows for some additional bonus features, such as function, intersection, and union types becoming possible – we'll come back to these later.

JavaScript Types Are Structural Contracts

Happily, JavaScript is structurally typed. But confusingly, it does this by using *runtime* typing of values, only asserting them when a value is required:

Listing 3-3. JavaScript runtime typing

```
function addToBoxInJavaScript(thing /* can pass anything in
                                       here */) {
  // No requirements up here
  console.log(`Adding ${thing}`);

  // JavaScript's runtime structural type assertion
  // happens here:
  // the minimum contract of height & width are asserted at
  // retrieval
  const height = thing.height;
  const width = thing.width;

  // Maybe further requirements down here
  // ...etc...
}
```

You can pass any value into the function in the preceding JavaScript code snippet, and the JavaScript runtime will only assert the value meets the "minimum contract" of the type when the code evaluates a code line where the value is further interrogated.

Allowing for structural typing is powerful, but JavaScript's do-it-at-runtime provision of this makes it tricky to refactor, as the runtime structural contracts become buried in the code, adding cognitive load.

TypeScript provides a way to specify these underlying runtime structural contracts as explicit up-front lint assertions, inline, within your JavaScript code. These TypeScript types thereby allow easier static analysis – thus simpler refactoring and thereby aiding your velocity when working at scale.

Adding Explicit Types to JavaScript

TypeScript is based on ECMAScript, providing a way to add inline lint annotation for the structural contracts – TypeScript is just JavaScript with type assertions added inline. And so, all the TypeScript compiler needs to do – aside from the hard work of asserting the structural contracts – is strip out the type lint, and the code is then valid JavaScript for normal use, bundling, etc. (In practice, the TypeScript compiler does a fair bit more than this, but it's a good mental model for now.)

Let's have a look at a very simple example:

Listing 3-4. A simple const

```
const fortyTwo = 42;
```

If you hover over the variable "fortyTwo" in your editor, you'll see a tooltip containing this:

Listing 3-5. TypeScript's analysis of our const

```
❯    const fortyTwo: 42
```

In the tooltip, the ": 42" suffix isn't the value – it's actually the TypeScript type constraint. Because we've used a constant, TypeScript is saying that the *only* value that is the right shape for this box is the value 42 itself. Let's try the same thing manually with a nonconstant by entering the following in our editor instead:

Listing 3-6. An equivalent let literal instead

```
let fortyTwo: 42 = 42;
```

This works. Now, if you try to assign the value again, it'll only work if the value assigned matches the "minimum contract" of our type constraint:

Listing 3-7. Attempting to reassign our constrained let literal

```
let fortyTwo: 42 = 42;
fortyTwo = 42; ✔ // fits the contract, so this doesn't error
fortyTwo = 58; ✗ // whereas here we're protected from the
                 // invalid value
```

This preceding narrow type constraint is called a "literal" type – a type whose value is *literally* the same as the type definition. These literal types can be used with all primitives:

Listing 3-8. Other primitive literals

```
// boolean literal types:
let yes: true = true;
let no: false = false;

// string literal types:
let red: '#990000' = '#990000';
```

We can also loosen (a.k.a. "widen") these structural constraints a bit too. The following allows the variable "age" to be assigned anything that is a number (therefore, it is no longer a literal type):

Listing 3-9. Widening our constraints

```
let age: number = 42;
age = 58; ✔ // yay! doesn't error
age = 'hello'; ✘ // phew, still protected from non-numbers
```

The same goes for other types:

Listing 3-10. Widening our constraints using other types

```
// boolean value types:
let isArchived: boolean = false;
isArchived = true; ✔ // doesn't error

// string value types:
let color: string = '#990000';
color = '#333333'; ✔ // doesn't error

// variable-length arrays:
const names: string[] = [ 'Ashley', 'Ted', 'Kim', 'Dave' ]; ✔
names[0] = 'Veronica'; ✔
names[0] = 42; ✘
```

So structural types allow us to specify that *only* values that fulfill the minimum contract of the type specified can be assigned. This isn't limited to primitives as shown in previous examples; we can also define custom shapes.

We can define a custom array, like this:

Listing 3-11. Custom arrays

```
// fixed-type array:
const values: [number, number, string, ...string[]] =
    [41, 32, 'hi']; ✔
values[0] = 4; ✔
values[8] = 9; ✘
values[8] = 'something'; ✔

// fixed-length array, also known as a 'tuple' (pronounced
    tuh-pl):
const coords: [number, number] = [41, 32]; ✔
coords[0] = 38; ✔
coords[8] = 14; ✘
```

And we can even define a custom object type, like this:

Listing 3-12. Custom object types

```
interface Employee {
    name: string
    employeeNumber: number
    dateOfBirth: Date
    address: {
      street: string
      postcode: string
    }
    isArchived: boolean
}
```

Once defined, we can use our custom object type to add a structural contract to a value like this:

Listing 3-13. Using our types as structural contracts

```
✔ // doesn't error
const amy: Employee = {
    name: "Amy",
    employeeNumber: 123,
    dateOfBirth: new Date(2000, 9, 1),
    address: {
        street: "123 Street",
        postcode: 1234
    },
    isArchived: false
}
✗ // this will error
const ted: Employee = {
    name: "Ted",
    employeeNumber: 123
}
```

In this way, structural contracts allow us to define the **minimum structure** that is required for value assignment.

This method of using types to define the minimum structure required can be used in other places too, such as function parameters:

Listing 3-14. Using TypeScript on function parameters

```
// Simple parameters:
function greet(firstName: string, lastName: string): string;
// or, using a lambda style:
// const greet = (firstName: string, lastName: string):
string => ...;

greet("Ted", "Smith") ✔ // doesn't error
greet(12345, "Smith") ✘ // this will error

// And complex parameters:
function draw(shape: {
    type: string, coords: [number, number] }): void;
// or, using a lambda style:
// const draw = (shape: {
    type: string, coords: [number, number] }) void => ...;

draw({
    type: 'square',
    coords: [32, 48]
}); ✔ // doesn't error

draw({
    type: 'square',
    coords: 'top left'
}); ✘ // this will error
```

Optionality

In the preceding **Employee** type, we might have one or two fields that we want to specify the type of *only* if they are present. We call these optional fields. We can use a shorthand "**?**" optionality modifier to indicate them:

Listing 3-15. Allowing some fields to be optional

```
interface Employee {
    name: string
    employeeNumber: number
    dateOfBirth?: Date       👉 // Optional
    address?: {              👉 // Optional
        street: string
        postcode: string
    }
    isArchived?: boolean     👉 // Optional
}
✔ // doesn't error
const amy: Employee = {
    name: "Amy",
    employeeNumber: 123
}

✘ // this will error
const ted: Employee = {
    name: "Ted",
    employeeNumber: 123,
    dateOfBirth: 'August'
}
```

This allows us to skip some fields if left undefined – while also ensuring that if they are present, they are the right type.

And we can use this optionality modifier in function definitions and class constructors too:

Listing 3-16. Allowing some parameters to be optional

```
// Optional function parameters
function greet(name: string, age?: number): string;
```

```
✔ // both these are fine:
greet('Homer', 42);
greet('Marge');
```

```
// Optional constructor parameters
class Person {
    constructor(name: string, email?: string, age?: number);
}
```

```
✔ // all these are fine:
new Person('John', 'john@example.com', 31);
new Person('Fi', 'fi@example.com');
new Person('Jane');
```

If you've got sharp eyes, you will have spotted that the optional parameters in the preceding examples are only ever trailing parameters. This is because the parameters are provided by calling code "ordinally" (in sequence), rather than by name – and so it would be impossible to write valid calling code that worked for the following:

Listing 3-17. Optional parameters have to be last

```
// The following will error...
function greet(name: string, age?: number, dob: Date): string; ✘
```

```
// ...because it's impossible to know if the following is
// correct or a typo:
greet('John', new Date()); 😟
```

Therefore, optional parameters must always be at the end of the function call, and so TypeScript includes a check for this as part of the type analysis.

All The Sugar

Over time, ECMAScript has added additional syntactic sugar to simplify common or complex tasks. And for all the ECMAScript features, TypeScript includes support for inferring their types out of the box. Let's pause for a moment and look at some of the more advanced ECMAScript features to explore the extent of the type safety TypeScript offers.

Array and Object Destructuring, Spread, and Rest

TypeScript provides type safety for array and object destructuring by analyzing the structure of the destructured variables and inferring their types from the matching types of the original objects or arrays, even using the ECMAScript rest operator (a.k.a. "...").

Listing 3-18. Destructuring arrays and object types

```
// For arrays:
const [name, age, ...others] = ["John", 30, true, "Red"];
❯    const name: string;
❯    const age: number;
❯    const others: [boolean, string];
```

```
// For objects:
const { name, age, ...others } =
   { name: "John", age: 30, isActive: true, color: "Red" };
❯    const name: string;
❯    const age: number;
❯    const others: { isActive: boolean, color: string };
```

Did you notice that TypeScript infers the preceding destructured values as nonliterals (e.g., **string**, **boolean**, **number**, etc.), rather than as the literals as we had in our original "const" example we started with? That's because, although the outer variable is a constant, the inner array items or object fields could be reassigned – so essentially it is like they are assigned with **let**. Instead, we can assign them as **const**, and the result is more expected:

Listing 3-19. Destructuring arrays and object types more narrowly

```
// For arrays:
const [name, age, ...others] =
    ["John", 30, true, "Red"] as const;
❯    const name: "John";
❯    const age: 30;
❯    const others: [true, "Red"];

// For objects:
const { name, age } =
   { name: "John", age: 30, isActive: true, color: "Red" }
   as const;
❯    const name: "John";
❯    const age: 30;
❯    const others: { isActive: true, color: "Red" };
```

This works for the spread on the assignee side too:

Listing 3-20. Types can be persisted even through spreads

```
// For arrays:
const lettersArray = ['b2', 'c3', 'd4', 'e5'] as const;
const newLettersArray = ['a1', ...lettersArray, 'f6'] as const;
>    const newLettersArray: readonly [
     "a1", "b2", "c3", "d4", "e5", "f6"];

// For objects:
const lettersObject = { b: 'b2', c: 'c3', d: 'd4', e: 'e5' }
as const;
const newLettersObject = { a: 'a1', ...lettersObject, f: 'f6' }
as const;
>    const newLettersObject: {
         readonly a: "a1", readonly b: "b2", readonly c: "c3",
         readonly d: "d4", readonly e: "e5", readonly f: "f6",
     };
```

🔅 Tuple destructuring in types is a technique we use in Chapter 6.
See **Flatten** and **UrlParameters** for examples.

These spread and rest operators work for type safety in function parameters too:

Listing 3-21. Type safety in spread and rest operators

```
function log(destination: string, ...values: string[]): void;

const lettersArray = ['a1', 'b2', 'c3', 'd4'];
const numbersArray = [1, 2, 3, 4];
log('letters', ...lettersArray); ✔ // This works fine
log('letters', ...numbersArray); ✗ // Throws an error,
                                   // as expected
```

However, you may find the readonly type assigned by the const keyword to be restrictive, especially if you need to pass your resultant tuple to a third-party library that isn't as strict in its input definitions. If you hit this annoying feature, you can take the following approach:

Listing 3-22. Loosening tuples for third-party interop

```
// Say you have a 3rd-party lib that takes a string[].
// It should take'readonly string[]', but they haven't typed
// it as strictly as that. (Most 3rd-party libraries are like
// this at present).
function thirdPartyLibMethod(values: string[]);

// If you try passing a native tuple to it, you will get
an error:
const nativeTuple = ['a', 'b', 'c'] as const;
thirdPartyLibMethod(nativeTuple); ✗ // Error: 'readonly
                                     string[]' and
                                     // string[] are not
                                     compatible ☹
```

```
// Solution: LooseTuple utility type
type LooseTuple<Values extends readonly any[]> = {
    -readonly [Key in keyof Values]: Values[Key]
};

function tuple<T extends readonly any[]>(values: T):
LooseTuple<T> {
    return values;
}

const looseTuple = tuple(['a', 'b', 'c'] as const);
```
›   *const looseTuple: ['a', 'b', 'c']*   🖘 not readonly

```
thirdPartyLibMethod(looseTuple);   ✔ // Works as expected ☺
```

Async

Modern ECMAScript and JavaScript also support async functions. These functions use the **await** keyword to return a **Promise** to their calling function and pass the remainder of their function body to the underlying JavaScript event loop to process when required resources are next allocatable.

And so, TypeScript includes native support for these **async** and **await** keywords and their **Promise** return values – allowing you to use structural types for these operators too:

Listing 3-23. Async functions

```
async function getPerson(id: number): Promise<Person> {
    // Code to load a person's data from an API
}

const mary = await getPerson(42);
```
›   *const mary: Person;*   // TypeScript knows **await** unwraps
                         // the Promise, so the type of **mary**
                         // is Person.

Generators

Lastly, generator functions in JavaScript allow you to yield values during iteration. You can think of them as working as if they had multiple successive return statements; although in reality when a generator function is called, it returns an iterator object, whose next, return, and throw methods are then used to simulate a sequence of values that the function yields.

Generator functions in ECMAScript (and therefore JavaScript) are defined using the **function*** syntax, – similar to the usual function keyword but with an asterisk (*) added after it. Inside the generator function, one then uses the **yield** keyword to emit a value and pause the execution of the function until the next value is requested.

TypeScript allows us to assign types to the returned **Generator** objects and thereby ensure type safety in calling code.

Listing 3-24. Generator functions

```
function* createEnumerable(count: number): Generator<number,
void, undefined> {
    for (let i = 0; i < count; i++) {
        yield i;
    }
}

for (const value of createEnumerable(5)) {
>    const value: number;
}
```

These generator functions can be coupled with async functionality to create highly efficient code:

Listing 3-25. Async generator functions

```
async function* loadPeople(count: number):
  AsyncGenerator<Person, void, unknown> {
    const people: Person[] = await (
      await fetch('/my-api/people?count=' + count)).json();
    for (const person of people) {
        yield person;
    }
    // nb: you can also use 'yield* people;' in place of the
    above loop
}

for await (const person of loadPeople(5)) {
>    const person: Person;
}
```

Inferred Types

Now that we've explored structural types through primitives and interfaces in TypeScript, let's get back into the types and how they work. To do this, we need to briefly review a powerful feature we touched on near the start: type inference, widening, and narrowing.

Types, Automagically

As you may have noticed, we don't have to add the actual types to our code for TypeScript to already be able to work out what type a value is. This is called **type inference**:

Listing 3-26. Automagically inferring types from their values

```
// TypeScript infers that a can only be the value 1, so it
// internally stores the type of a as 1:
const a = 1;
>    type a: 1;
```

```
// TypeScript infers here that b is a number, but may not only
// be 1 because (as a let) it may be reassigned, - so it
// internally stores the type of b as number:
let b = 1;
>    type b: number;
```

```
// As we saw before when destructuring arrays, TypeScript can
// infer the type of an array...
const c = [1, 2, 3];
>    type c: number[];
```

```
// ...and when we append the special as const modifier, it'll
// infer the value exactly instead...
const d = [1, 2, 3] as const;
>    type d: readonly [1, 2, 3];
```

```
// ...right down to the individually extracted values...
const [_, e, ...restOfD] = d;
>    type e: 2;
```

```
// ...and the directly referenced values:
const f = d[2];
>    type f: 3;
```

```
// However, TypeScript isn't smart enough yet to infer
// 'type g: 3', but it goes for the next-best alternative if it
// can't infer a value fully:
const g = c + 1;
```
➤   *type g: number;*

```
// Even though we haven't specified a return type, TypeScript
// uses the function's return statement to work out what the
// return type is...
function greet(name: string) /* no return type specified */ {
    return `Hello ${name}!`;
}
```
➤   *type greet: (name: string) => string;*

```
// ...and so it can use that return type here:
const greeting = greet('Felicity');
```
➤   *type greeting: string;*

```
// Even function parameters can be inferred from their
// default values:
function greet(name: string, salutation = 'Hello') {
```
➤   *type salutation: string;*
```
    return `${salutation} ${name}!`;
}
```

```
/* TypeScript can also use the context of a value to deduce
its type. Here the type of the event args is inferred from the
event we are attaching this function to: */
document.onmousemove = function (event) {
```

```
❯    type event: MouseEvent;
   console.log(event.clientX);   ✔ // This works fine
   console.log(event.foo);       ✘ // Throws an error
                                   because .foo doesn't
}                                  // exist on the inferred
                                   MouseEvent type

function registerLogger(logger: (s: string) => void);

// Using a similar strategy, TypeScript infers that the type
// of s is string because that's what the callsite's context
// would require:
registerLogger(
    (s) => console.log(s)
❯    type s: string;
);

// TypeScript can even infer generic parameters from their
// supplied values! (nb: I'm jumping ahead a bit here - we'll
// cover this last one in Chapter 5: Computed Types)
function createList<const T>(items: Array<T>): { items:
Array<T> };
const list = createList(['Red', 'Blue', 'Green']);
❯    type list: {
        items: ("Red" | "Blue" | "Green")[];
     }
```

💡 TypeScript also has some additional advanced keywords to help infer types – we'll circle back to these in Chapter 5.

Type Widening and Narrowing

Type inference may seem a handy shorthand at this point – and it is. But it also is a great way to keep types as constrained as possible, by getting the compiler to infer the types automagically for you. This helps with maintenance too as well as helps constrain progressive states of variables within a code block. But to really find the benefit of this in our code, we'll need to go deeper to understand an underlying superpower feature of TypeScript: type widening and narrowing.

In brief, type widening refers to where a type is made **less** strict than the value initially assigned. This can occur automatically, or can be explicitly specified. For example:

Listing 3-27. Widening a type with let vs. const

```
// We know that the type of 'age' will be inferred as a literal
// type, 42:
const age = 42;
❯    const age: 42

// But using 'let', the compiler automatically widens the type
// to number...
let age = 42;
❯    let age: number
```

43

```
// ...because otherwise there would be no point having it as a
// 'let' because without this auto-widening, no other value
// could be assigned:
age = 32; ✔ // yay, this is ok!
```

You can also explicitly widen a type yourself, too, if you like:

Listing 3-28. Widening a type using an explicit type, in this case, a union

```
// Automatically widened:
let age = 40;
  >    let age: number

// Manually widened, explicitly setting a smaller type:
let age: 20 | 30 | 40 = 40; // for details, see section on
                            // union types
  >    let age: 20 | 30 | 40
```

Conversely, type narrowing refers to where a type can be used as a type **more** strict than initially defined. It, too, can occur automatically, or can be explicitly specified. For example:

Listing 3-29. Narrowing a type using assertions and casts

```
// Automatically narrowed:
function convertToString(o: object) {
    if (o instanceof Date) {
        // If the runtime reaches this point, TypeScript infers
        // that 'o' will have all the methods available on a
        // 'Date' object, and so automatically narrows the value
        // to be a 'Date' type here:
```

```
        return o.toUTCString();
    >       (parameter) o: Date
    }
    // ...etc
}

// Manually narrowed:
const inputElement = document.getElementById('my-input') as
HTMLInputElement;
/* (the 'as' keyword allows us to specify to the compiler
that we know that the 'my-input' element will always be an
HTMLInputElement, rather than the less-specific Element type
normally returned by getElementById) */
```

Auto-narrowing, but Not Too Much

As types represent structural "minimum contracts," TypeScript will also allow explicit and automatic narrowing of types such as the following:

Listing 3-30. Manual and auto-narrowing by using types

```
const ted = {
    firstName: 'Ted',
    lastName: 'Smith',
    age: 28,
    favorites: {
        color: 'red',
        icecream: 'choc chip'
    }
}
```

```
// Example 1: explicitly narrowing by assigning ted to a more
// narrow type
interface Person {
    firstName: string
    lastName: string
    age: number
}

// This is ok, because 'ted' fulfills the minimum fields
// required by the'Person' type.
const p: Person = ted; ✔ // value of ted is narrowed to the
                            Person type

// ...and, Example 2: explicitly narrowing by assigning to a
// function param that covers the same core required field of
// 'firstName':
interface Greetable {
    firstName: string
}
function greet(greetable: Greetable): void;

// This, too, is ok - because 'ted' fulfills the minimum fields
// required by the Greetable type
greet(ted); ✔ // value of ted is narrowed to the
                Greetable type
```

However, early in TypeScript, this was also found to allow accidental typos too, for example:

Listing 3-31. Structural types, if left as simple "minimum contracts," could permit typos

```
interface Person {
    firstName: string
    lastName: string
    age?: number // <- optional field
}

// If we followed a naive approach of 'minimal contract only',
// the following would be acceptable, because 'age' is optional
// in the Person type, and our typo would not cause an error.
const tedAsPerson: Person = {
    firstName: 'Ted',
    lastName: 'Smith',
    ageeeee: 28,
}; ✔ // <- ⚠ oh no, this should've raised an error, but
        // it doesn't
```

So TypeScript was also given one special case to cover the need illustrated in the preceding example: "TS2322 Object literal may only specify known properties." This special case added a logic path to the compiler asserting that when specifying a new inline value where an

explicit type is stated, it must not have any fields outside of the type stated.
And so TypeScript now guards against this issue in the following, more
helpful, way:

Listing 3-32. Auto-narrowing includes a special case to
prevent typos

```
// Example 1: narrowing not permitted because of new value vs
// explicit type
interface Person {
    firstName: string
    lastName: string
    age?: number // <- optional field
}
const tedAsPerson: Person = {
    firstName: 'Ted',
    lastName: 'Smith',
    ageeeee: 28, ✗ // Yay! a helpful error, alerting us to
                    the typo
};

// Example 2: narrowing not permitted because of new value vs
// explicit type
interface Greetable {
    firstName: string
}
function greet(person: Greetable): void;

greet({
    firstName: 'Ted',
    lastName: 'Smith', ✗ // A helpful error here, alerting us
                        // to extra param
})
```

Type Assertions

Assertions are a way to tell the compiler more information about the type of a variable than it can infer on its own. In the majority of cases, you should avoid this, but there are cases where you are interacting with a safe, known state that can help to share your external understanding of a system with the compiler. Here's an example of a simple assertion on a value:

Listing 3-33. Explicit types switch type checking back on again for the value

```
const value = await fetch(`/person/${personId}');
>    const value: any;

/* Maybe, because I know the API is completely reliable, I
know that the type of the returned value will always match our
Person type exactly, and so I can just assert that the value is
this type: */

const person: Person = value;
>    const person: Person;
console.log(person.name); // After the cast, we get type-safety
```

We've used the approach in the preceding example before, defining the types of variables. This is known as a compile-time assertion. In this section, we'll cover the two types of assertions you can use: both compile-time and runtime.

Compile-Time Assertions

Compile-time assertions check and augment the types of your values before the program runs. They are removed by the compiler before runtime. Let's look at them now.

as Keyword

The **as** keyword allows us to tell TypeScript that a value is of a particular type. This is commonly known as *casting*, and it is by this name this process is often called in TypeScript. But this isn't actually accurate.

In most languages, you can freely cast from one type to another. But as you could guess, this is equivalent to overriding type checking and, if permitted in TypeScript, could lead to all sorts of runtime errors. So to protect against this, TypeScript goes beyond traditional type *casting* to a slightly more refined programmatic translation called *type coercion*.

Type coercion is the translation of one type to another. Using this, TypeScript can determine that impossible coercions can be raised as errors. For example:

Listing 3-34. TypeScript asserts casts are viable – here's a case that is not possible

```
interface Person {
    firstName: string
    lastName: string
}

interface HTMLElement {
    nodeName: string
}
```

```
// Not permitted, because there is no way an HTMLElement type
// overlaps with a Person type:
const jim = document.getElementById('jim') as Person; ✘
```

Because an **HTMLElement** does not fulfill the minimum requirements of the shape required by **Person** (remember: types are minimum contracts – see the "Structural Typing" section), TypeScript does not permit the coercion. And in this way, TypeScript provides more safety than traditional casting.

Listing 3-35. TypeScript asserts casts are viable – here's a case that is possible

```
interface Person {
    name: string
}

interface Employee {
    name: string
    employeeNumber: number
    department: string
}

const employee123: Employee = {
    name: 'Jim',
    employeeNumber: 123,
    department: 'Shipping',
}

// Permitted, because the Employee and Person types are
// compatible
const jim = employee123 as Person; ✔
```

However, type coercion checks in TypeScript are not perfect, and so the **as** keyword still needs to be used with caution. If there is enough overlap between the types, TypeScript will allow it (because there are valid scenarios that require this), but it can also lead to logic issues as shown in the following code:

Listing 3-36. TypeScript asserts casts are viable – but watch out for accidental overlaps

```
interface Cat {
    name: string
}

// Employee type overlaps partially with Cat type, so this is
// permitted 😵
const myCat = employee123 as Cat; ✔ ⚠ // <- Danger
```

Happily, there are better ways to include data in a type than often using the **as** keyword. We'll cover a few of these in the other assertions, but check out the "Union Types" section in Chapter 5 too, as that's the most powerful approach to take.

satisfies Keyword

Assigning types to variables brings us type safety, but sometimes, it can also obscure tighter types that could be inferred. Take the following example:

Listing 3-37. Assigning a simple explicit type

```
interface Person {
    name: string
    age: number
    address?: {
```

```
        street: string
        postcode?: string
    },
}
const jim: Person = {
    name: 'Jim',
    age: 43
}
```

Using the **Person** type for the **jim** variable, we get type safety. But looking more closely, we see that TypeScript now infers the variable as follows:

Listing 3-38. Using explicit types can lose important detail

```
const jim
❯    const jim: Person {
        name: string
        age: number
        address?: {
            street: string
            postcode?: string
        }
    };
```

And in our IDE, our intellisense reflects Figure 3-5.

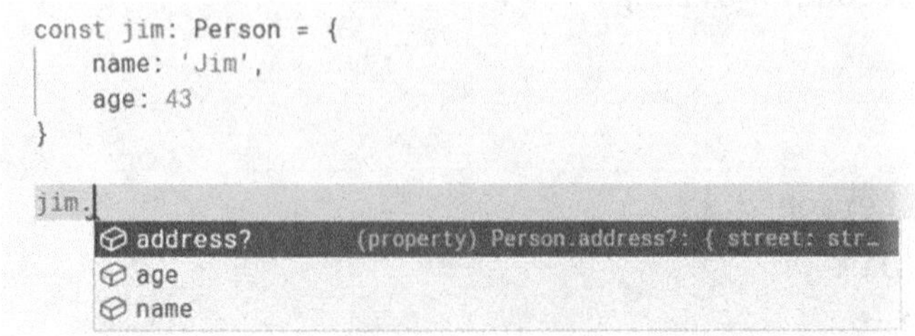

```
const jim: Person = {
    name: 'Jim',
    age: 43
}

jim.
    ⊘ address?        (property) Person.address?: { street: str…
    ⊘ age
    ⊘ name
```

Figure 3-5. *Intellisense shows the field, even though the value doesn't have it*

This is not particularly helpful – especially as we can see that the value doesn't have an address field. So, what can we do about it? This is where the **satisfies** keyword comes in. Instead of marking the variable as a type, we can instead specify that the variable only **satisfies** the minimum contract provided by a type and is otherwise in its own shape:

Listing 3-39. Using inferred types keeps the detail intact

```
const jim = {
    name: 'Jim',
    age: 43,
} satisfies Person;

>    const jim: {
        name: string
        age: number
     };
```

But let's go a bit better, as discussed in the "Structural Typing" section:

Listing 3-40. Use a tighter inferred type to keep even more detail

```
const jim = {
    name: 'Jim',
    age: 43,
} as const satisfies Person;

>    const jim: {
        readonly name: "Jim"
        readonly age: 43
     };
```

And the IDE experience is more useful too (Figure 3-6).

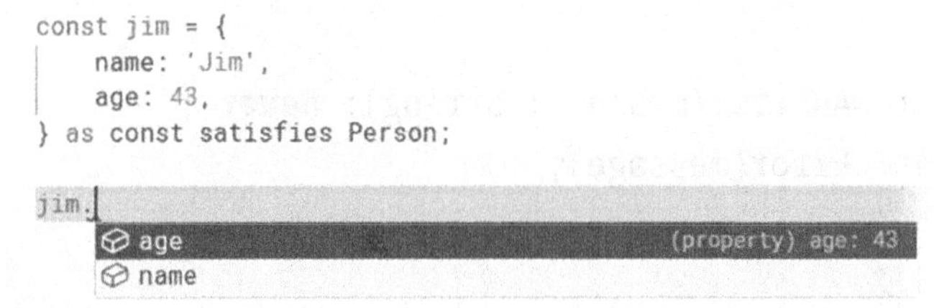

Figure 3-6. *Intellisense shows only the fields applicable to the value*

never Keyword

Last of the compile-time assertions is the **never** keyword. This keyword allows us to state that a type can never be true. "Wait – what?" I hear you say. When would we use such a type? In practice, this type allows for some powerful assertions: exhaustivity checking and invalid return assertion.

Take a look at this function as an example. I've left off the return type. What should I set it as?

Listing 3-41. What is the return type of a function that cannot complete?

```
function throwAnError(message: string) {
    throw new Error(message);
}
```

In the preceding snippet, the function will *never* return a value – it will always throw an error. Therefore, for the function's return type, we use the special TypeScript type, **never**:

Listing 3-42. The return type of a function that cannot complete is never

```
function throwAnError(message: string): never {
    throw new Error(message);
}
```

Marking the return type as **never** allows the compiler to assert that statements following the return are logically unreachable and therefore could be an error:

Listing 3-43. TypeScript's control-flow analysis recognizes statements after a never as unreachable

```
throwAnError('This is an error');

console.log('This will never be logged'); ⚠ // Warning:
                                             // unreachable
                                             // code
```

This first way is a helpful way to instruct the compiler on logic flow, but the second way is even more useful: the use of the **never** keyword is for exhaustivity checking. Take the following example:

Listing 3-44. Using a switch statement against a finite set of possible values

```
enum Color {
    red,
    blue,
    green,
}

function log(color: Color, message: string): void {
    switch (color) {
        case Color.red:
            console.log('#ff0000', message);
            break;
        case Color.blue:
            console.log('#0000ff', message);
            break;
        case Color.green:
            console.log('#00ff00', message);
            break;
    }
}
```

Aside from the mistake of using enums in the preceding example (seriously: never use enums – use **union types** instead), there's another maintenance risk: What if someone updates the Color type to include another color? They'll have to search for every usage of Color within our system to make sure that it has been accounted for. Does this sound like a maintenance nightmare to you, too?

Instead, the never type allows us to assert that we have covered all cases in our function by including a default case and checking that the value is coercible to never:

Listing 3-45. Using never to ensure our switch statement is maintainable

```
enum Color {
    red,
    blue,
    green,
    magenta,     ✑ // Added a new value here
}

function assertIsNever(n: never): never {
    // ...
}

function log(color: Color, message: string): void {
    switch (color) {
        case Color.red:
            console.log('#ff0000', message);
            break;
        case Color.blue:
            console.log('#0000ff', message);
            break;
        case Color.green:
            console.log('#00ff00', message);
            break;
```

```
    default:
        assertIsNever(color); ✗ /* TS now helpfully flags
                                   here that the newly added
                                   case is not covered. */

    }
}
```

Then, when we add a color to our enum (or extend our planned union type), the compiler will mark that the value is no longer coercible to never, and we can easily update our code.

Runtime Assertions

Runtime assertions check the shape of your values while your program is running; and their checks can be computed back into compile-time by TypeScript to add pre-build checks too. We'll cover them in detail in the following subsections.

typeof, instanceof, and in Operators

ECMAScript, and therefore JavaScript, includes the **typeof**, **instanceof**, and **in** operator keywords. These allow JavaScript developers to check the shape of values at runtime, and so TypeScript can use these to automatically narrow types (see the preceding Inferred Types section entitled **Type Widening and Narrowing**) accordingly.

(Note: You may also see a **typeof** keyword used in type computation and inference – although spelt the same, this is actually a different keyword, and you can find details of it in the "Inferred Types" section in Chapter 5, farther on in this book).

The data types in ECMAScript include primitive types such as boolean, number, bigint, string, function, and symbol, and the nonprimitive type object. The **typeof** operator keyword returns which of these types a variable currently is. Therefore, TypeScript can use this operator to infer the type of a value within a conditional check such as shown in the following code:

Listing 3-46. The typeof operator keyword allows runtime assertions that TypeScript can use to narrow the type

```
function write(answer: any) {
    if (typeof answer === 'string') {
        // Within this if, TypeScript will infer 'answer' is a
        // string,...
        console.log(`You answered: ${answer.toUpperCase()}`);
    }
    else if (typeof answer === 'number') {
        // ...in this if that 'answer' is a number,...
        console.log(`You answered: ${answer.toPrecision(2)}`);
    }
    else if (typeof answer === 'boolean') {
        // ...and in this if that 'answer' is a boolean.
        console.log(`You answered: ${answer === true ? 'Yes' :
        'No'}`);
    }
    else {
        throw new Error(`Unrecognized type: ${typeof answer}`);
    }
}
```

The ECMAScript **instanceof** operator is used to check whether an object is an instance of a specific class or parent class. Therefore, TypeScript can use it similarly to the **typeof** operator to determine a value's shape when it's type is "object":

Listing 3-47. The instanceof operator keyword also allows runtime assertions that TypeScript can use to narrow the type

```
function write(answer: any) {
    // ...
    else if (typeof answer === 'object') {
        if (answer instanceof Date) {
            // In this condition, TypeScript will know 'answer'
            // is a Date...
            console.log(`You answered: ${answer.
            toISOString()}`);
        }
        else if (answer instanceof Array) {
            // ...here it will know it is an Array...
            console.log(`You answered: ${answer.join(',')}`);
        }
        else if (answer instanceof MyCustomClass) {
            // ...and here it is our custom class, or a
            // subclass thereof.
            console.log(`You answered: ${answer.getValue()}`);
        }
    }

    // ...
}
```

Finally, in ECMAScript, the **in** operator is used to check if an object contains a given field, and so TypeScript can use this to infer the type too:

Listing 3-48. The instanceof operator keyword also allows runtime assertions that TypeScript can use to narrow the type

```
function write(answer: any) {
    // ...
    else if (typeof answer === 'object') {
        // ...
        else if (
            'someMethod' in answer
            && typeof answer.someMethod === 'function'
        ) {
            // We don't know the type, but we can still assert
            // the value has a known method we can call.
            console.log(`You answered; ${answer.
            someMethod()}`);
        }
        // ...
    }

    // ...
}
```

Custom Assertions

You can also write your own custom assertions, which wrap complex checks in simple-to-use functions. To do so, these functions return a **type predicate**, using a special **is** keyword as shown in the following example:

Listing 3-49. Using a TypeScript type predicate function

```
function isStringArray(o: any): o is string[] {        🖘
    // Type predicate...
    return (
        typeof o === 'object'
        && o instanceof Array
        && o.every(item => typeof item === 'string')
    );
}

function uppercaseArray(o: any): string[] {
    if (!isStringArray(o)) {        🖘 // ...and its usage.
        throw new Error('Requires a string array');
    }
    // Because of the type predicate function above, by this
    // point in the code TypeScript knows that every item in
    // the array is a string.
    return o.map(item => item.toUpperCase());
}
```

Existing Tools

Writing runtime assertions is possible, as seen in the preceding example, and whenever interacting with errors and APIs, it is necessary. But it can also be repetitive and has opportunities for errors. Happily, there are now several libraries that can do this for you and that provide type assertions back to TypeScript to use. Of the available libraries, one of the more popular that aligns well with TypeScript's own types is **zod**.

Listing 3-50. Zod allows easy runtime validations that return typed values

```
import { z } from 'zod';

// In Zod you define the type as a runtime object, rather than
// in TypeScript
const personType = z.object({
    name: z.string(),
    age: z.number(),
    isActive: z.boolean(),
    address: z.object({
        street: z.string(),
        postcode: z.string().optional(),
    }).optional(),
})

// Zod allows you to infer the type back into TypeScript
type Person = z.TypeOf<typeof personType>;

// loadValue() may still return unknown, but now our personType
// can do all the runtime assertions for us.
const maybePerson = personType.safeParse(loadValue());
if (maybePerson.success) {
    // If 'success' is true, then 'data' contains the
    // safely parsed runtime value.
    console.log(maybePerson.data.name,
        maybePerson.data.address?.street);
}
```

There are several libraries like this available (**AJV**, **fp-ts**, **Joi**, **io-ts**, **Yup**, and others), and I would recommend experimenting with a few to find which ones fit your own needs best.

any and unknown Keywords

TypeScript gives us some amazing safety for propagating a variable's type through our code base. As shown in the preceding example, TypeScript can infer or allow explicit statement of structural types for variables and then also ensure that our interaction with the variables matches these types. But it can only do this where the type is actually known – where the value is created within our own program. So what can we do for times where the type cannot be known?

For example:

- When loading a value from an API call

- When reading an environment variable

- When interacting with a project written in JavaScript

In fact, all of the preceding cases can be condensed into the first case: When interacting with an external API, what should we specify that a returned value's type is?

The truth is we don't know what the returned value's shape is until we've checked it. And so for this, TypeScript includes two mechanisms to mark a type as needing further assertion before safe usage. These mechanisms are embedded in two keywords: **any** and **unknown**.

The **any** keyword gives a way to temporarily "switch off" TypeScript for a variable and say that it will be asserted at runtime. It can be used like this:

Listing 3-51. "any" switches off type checking for the value

```
const value: any = loadValue();

// TypeScript won't offer intellisense for fields on
// 'value', because by using 'any' we've essentially told it to
// skip type checks. So we can just reference fields
// dynamically, assuming instead external knowledge of the
// fields available at runtime.

value.foo = "";     ✔ // This is accepted...
value.bar(12, 34); ✔ // ...and so is this...
value.baz += true; ✔ // ...and this.
```

If we want to turn TypeScript back on for the variable, we need to cast it back to a known type:

Listing 3-52. Explicit types switch type checking back on again for the value

```
const value: any = loadValue();

const knownValue: Person = value;
knownValue.foo = ""; ✘ // Throws an error, as expected
```

Originally **any** was the only inbuilt type shipped with TypeScript that switched off the type checking, and so in some of the older libraries available on NPM, these are still present in return types. But turning off type checking in your APIs, when you've already explicitly decided to use a type checker in order to achieve the benefits already discussed, would be somewhat self-defeating. And so it was realized that what was often desired was not an unchecked type (**any**), but a type that couldn't be known yet and needed further assertions before use – and so the **unknown** type was added.

The **unknown** type works identically to the **any** type, with one major difference: it requires runtime assertion before the compiler will permit it to be used:

Listing 3-53. Narrowing an "unknown" using runtime assertions

```
const value: unknown = loadValue();

value.foo(); ✗ // Throws an error, as value is unknown
// However, if we do the exact same checks in code that
// TypeScript would otherwise do for us, then we can know that
// the value's shape is assertable, and therefore
if (
    typeof value === 'object'
    && value !== null
    && 'foo' in value
    && typeof value.foo === 'function'
) {
    // <- ...here this is fine :)
    value.foo(); ✓
}
```

Due to the way that ECMAScript's try/catch spec allows all values to be thrown as error data, it's usually best to assume that caught data is **unknown** and needs interrogation before use. The same is true for API responses (both local APIs and remote web APIs). These are the areas you are most likely to need to use the **unknown** type and perform these assertions.

And we'll look more deeply at type assertions next. But first a word of warning.

Caution: Handle with Care

Obviously, using the **any** and **unknown** keywords to switch off TypeScript's checks, even temporarily, leads to bugs and maintenance overheads. So we want to do so sparingly. But in this book, we're going to go deeper than the basics, and in doing so, sometimes, there will be times you will know more than the compiler can infer. In fact, Figure 3-7 shows a completely unscientific but I'd dare say accurate graph of the number of times you use these keywords as you gain familiarity with TypeScript.

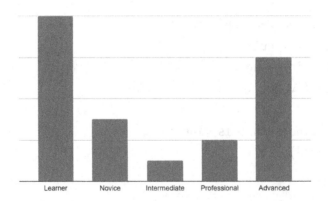

Figure 3-7. *Illustrative of the number of any types you may end up using*

The point I'm making here is that when learning, you may need to use **any** and **unknown** lots of times, as you battle through reconciling types. After gaining familiarity, using this book, you'll start to see more and more opportunities to use features such as mapped and conditional types to help protect your code, and hopefully will begin aiming for a "near-zero-anys" policy in your code – and this is an admirable aim. But don't be concerned if, once you start to master the language, you also find there are times you need to augment TypeScript's ability to interpret the types with any or unknown, internally – within safely localized code, where the values are known. But try not to expose **any** as a public return type: you will usually be able to give consumers of your code more data about a value than that – as we'll explore in the rest of this book.

Parameterized Values

The types that we've covered so far are all for unparameterized values – variables that return a data value directly, without requiring runtime parameters, for example:

Listing 3-54. These values return data directly, without requiring runtime parameters

```
const n = 1;               // n is assigned a number
const isAllowed = false;    // isAllowed is assigned a boolean
const employee1 = nancy;   // employee1 is assigned a Person
```

But ECMAScript (and therefore JavaScript) also specifies that some values need runtime parameters in order to supply a value. Here are three examples:

Listing 3-55. These values only return the data we need after we have provided runtime parameters

```
// color is assigned a hex color value
const color = colors['blue'];
// user is assigned a User
const tim = loadUser(123);
// dob is assigned a Date
const dob = new MyDate(2000, 5, 10);
```

However, previously we have only covered types that return values directly, like this:

Listing 3-56. An example of how we define a value that does not require runtime parameters to return data

```
interface Person {
    // Defining simple fields in an interface or type
    // is easy...
    firstName: string
    lastName: string
}
```

So how do we define types for those subjects on the right such as **colors[..]**, **loadUser(..)**, or **Date(..)**, as in the preceding example? How do we write types that take parameters before supplying a value? We will explore these now.

Index Signatures

Let's start with the easiest first: types that can take index values before providing a value. The following code is an example of this:

Listing 3-57. How do we define a type that takes an index parameter in order to return data?

```
const colors: ??? = {
    red: '#FF0000',
    green: '#00FF00',
    blue: '#0000FF',
    // ...etc...
};

const value = colors['blue']; ✏️  // Accessing via an index
❯    const value = '#0000FF';      // signature
dictionary['orange'] = '#FFA000'; // Setting via an index
                                  // signature
```

To specify that a type has an index signature, we define it like this:

Listing 3-58. Defining an interface that includes an index key type and its return type

```
interface ColorDictionary {
              👇 the type of the index's key
    [color: string]: string
                    👆 the type of the value which is
                       returned or set
}
```

```
const colors: ColorDictionary = {
    red: '#FF0000',
    green: '#00FF00',
    blue: '#0000FF',
    // ...etc...
};
```

The **ColorDictionary** interface in the preceding example code specifies that the value can receive any string in its index signature and will return a string value. You can also use union types in index signatures to constrain the index – see the "Union Types" section in Chapter 5.

💡 We use index signatures and union types in some of our advanced types created in Chapter 6. Have a look at the **JsonOf** and **UrlParameters** examples.

Function Signatures

Function signatures extend on index signatures and allow our value to take one or more parameters before computing and returning a result.

Listing 3-59. How do we define a type that needs function parameters in order to return data?

```
interface LoadUserFunction {
    // How do we write an interface or type for something
    // that would take parameters before returning a result?
}
```

```
const loadUser: LoadUserFunction = (userId: string) => {
    // ...
};
```

```
const tim = loadUser(123);
```

Happily, it's quite simple – similarly to index signatures, we just define the interface using parentheses **()** to hold the parameters:

Listing 3-60. Defining an interface that includes a function parameter and return type

```
interface LoadUserFunction {
    (usedId: number): User
}
```

```
const loadUser: LoadUserFunction = (userId) => {
    // ...
};
```

```
const tim = loadUser(123);
❯    const tim: User;
```

And if we need overloads, we can define those simply in the same type too:

Listing 3-61. Defining an interface that includes multiple (i.e., overloaded) function parameters and return type combinations

```
interface LoadUserFunction {
    (authToken: string): User
    (authToken: string, dataCenter: string,
        tenancyId: string): User
    (email: string, password: string): User
}
```

Constructor Signatures

Lastly, constructor signatures – how would we define an interface for something like the following code?

Listing 3-62. How do we define a type that we can pass constructor parameters to and will return a new instance?

```
interface MyDateConstructor {
    /* How do we specify parameters that will attach to
    ECMAScript's new keyword, and call the type's special
    constructor method? */
}

const dateConstructor: MyDateConstructor = MyDateClass;

const dob = new dateConstructor(2000, 5, 10);
```

Again, similarly to index signatures and function signatures, you can define a constructor for a type using parameters and indicating it with the **new** keyword:

Listing 3-63. Defining an interface that allows the "new" keyword to trigger a constructor

```
abstract class MyDateAbstractClass {}

interface MyDateConstructor {
    new (year: number, month: number, day: number):
        MyDateAbstractClass;
}

class MyDateClass {
    constructor(year, month, day) { }
}
```

```
const dateConstructor: MyDateConstructor = MyDateClass;

const dob = new dateConstructor(2000, 5, 10);
❯    const dot: MyDateAbstractClass;
```

Note   You'd probably only want to use this last type of interface
if you were needing to constrain a function parameter to a
constructable class, but it's worth seeing as part of the parameterized
values principle.

A New Mental Model

So I want to present what may be a new mental model for you here. Some
subjects in ECMAScript return values directly (fields, variables); others
require parameters before returning values (indexable types, functions,
constructors). But both types can be defined using TypeScript interfaces.

    And with this in mind, now here's the really interesting part in
ECMAScript. Functions in ECMAScript (and therefore JavaScript) are
objects. Take a look at the following valid ECMAScript/JavaScript code
example:

Listing 3-64. ECMAScript/JavaScript requires a new mental model
for types

```
const historyValues: string[] = [];
function f(n: string) {
    historyValues.push(n);
    return n.toUpperCase();
}
```

```
// In ECMAScript/JavaScript, functions are objects and
// therefore can also have values 🤯
f.history = historyValues;

const greeter: ??? = f;

greeter('hi');
greeter('bye');

const result = greeter.history;
>    const result = ['hi', 'bye'];
```

In the preceding example, the greeter function *both* takes parameters (as a function) *and* has simple fields! How would we type that?

Actually, TypeScript can even deal with this sort of craziness by just including both parameterized results and field results in the same interface:

Listing 3-65. ECMAScript/JavaScript types can have multiple parameterized and nonparameterized call options (simple example)

```
export interface SelfLoggingGreeter {
    (name: string): string
    history: string[]
}
```

```
const greeter: SelfLoggingGreeter = f;
```

In fact, because JavaScript allows this sort of thing (which might not be a good thing), TypeScript can cope with combining all the above signatures – parameterized and nonparameterized, in a single interface, as shown in the following extreme example:

Listing 3-66. ECMAScript/JavaScript types can have multiple parameterized and nonparameterized call options (advanced)

```
interface CrazyShape {
    // This crazy interface is both non-parameterised AND
    // parameterised...

    // Non-parameterised, containing...
    // ☺ ...a simple field...
    foo: string

    // ☺ ...and a simple field that takes params
    // (ie. a func)...
    bar: () => string

    // ...and parameterised, responding to...
    // 😲 ...an index signature...
    [key: string]: any

    // 😲 ...AND function params...
    (param1: string, param2: string): string
    // 🤯   ...with an overload...
    (param1: string, param2: string, param3: string): number

    // 😵 ...AND you can also call 'new CrazyShapeImpl(...)'
    // on it! Yikes!
    new (param1: string, param2: string): AbstractCrazyShape
}
```

Note   Please, please don't make something like this! 😆 The preceding example is only to demonstrate how TypeScript allows you to combine parameterized and nonparameterized signatures to cover all the eventualities possible in JavaScript.

Summary

In this chapter, we explored the concept of "structural typing" in TypeScript, also known as "duck typing," where the shape of an object's structure takes precedence over its specific type or class.

We compared structural typing with traditional polymorphism and inheritance, finding that structural types provide greater flexibility and scalability, avoiding the need for brittle class hierarchies. We saw that by defining a "minimum contract" for a value, TypeScript enables various objects to fulfill that contract, thereby embracing the dynamic nature of JavaScript while ensuring type safety.

Throughout the chapter, we learned how to add explicit types to JavaScript as pre-build lint using TypeScript. We explored how the power of structural typing, through examples, could simplify code and improve scalability. We learned about various TypeScript features, including custom types, array and object destructuring, spread, rest, optionality, async functions, and generators, understanding how TypeScript ensures type safety for each of these constructs.

We then delved into the fascinating world of type assertions, and widening and narrowing, where TypeScript automatically refines types based on context and conditions. We discussed compile-time and runtime type assertions using operators like typeof, instanceof, and in, and how to write custom type assertions using type predicates. And we explored important tools like **never** and **satisfies**, which provide explicit control-flow analysis and easier type narrowing, respectively.

At the same time, we discovered the importance of handling keywords like **any** and **unknown** with caution, using them sparingly, and striving to minimize their use over time to enhance code safety and maintainability, but understanding their place in advanced usage.

And lastly we explored a new way of looking at functions, indexables, and constructors as parameterized values and saw how TypeScript can – taking this new mental model – allow us to define the types of even these parameterized types in a structurally typed context.

By the end of this chapter, you will have a solid understanding of structural typing in TypeScript and how it empowers developers to achieve a balance between type safety and flexibility in their JavaScript projects, as well as how to now define any structural type to suit your own needs.

CHAPTER 4

Classes

Introduction

In this chapter, we will explore how to add TypeScript type safety to the central building block of object-oriented programming in JavaScript – namely, classes.

We'll begin by learning how to create classes in JavaScript and TypeScript, with type-safe constructors, access modifiers, fields, getters/setters, and methods; and we'll explore type-safe inheritance and interface implementation, and instance and static modifiers.

But while classes offer powerful abstractions for structuring code, it's essential to understand their limitations. And so the remainder of this chapter will discuss the important difference between classes and types in TypeScript and how using classes as types may lead to unexpected behavior. Additionally, we'll explore the concept of scope bleed, a common issue associated with classes, and review how these objects fit (or not) in a truly structurally typed context.

By the end of this chapter, you'll have a solid understanding of classes in TypeScript and how to use them wisely to create robust and scalable applications. Embracing classes alongside functional programming techniques understandingly will empower you to make well-informed decisions about how best to write code that is performant as well as maintainable and easily testable.

Let's dive in and explore the world of classes in TypeScript!

© Ben Beattie-Hood 2023
B. Beattie-Hood, *Modern TypeScript*, https://doi.org/10.1007/978-1-4842-9723-0_4

Classes

To create a class in ECMAScript or JavaScript, you simply use the **class** keyword and then also give it a **constructor**:

Listing 4-1. Defining a class in ECMAScript/JavaScript

```
class MyClass {
    constructor() {
        // ...
    }
}
```

Constructors

Constructors can have parameters, which, like function parameters, have their types defined inline:

Listing 4-2. Using types for class constructor parameters

```
class MyClass {
    constructor(myField: number) {
        // ...
    }
}
```

Access Modifiers

Access modifiers allow you to control the visibility and accessibility of class members. TypeScript supports three access modifiers: **private**, **protected**, and **public**.

- **private** members are only accessible within an instance of the class.

- **protected** members are accessible within an instance of the class and any subclasses.

- **public** members are accessible on an instance of the class from anywhere.

Fields

There's literally zero point having a class if it doesn't have **state** – you'd be better off providing the functionality as a set of top-level functions. Class state is held in fields, and in TypeScript, these can be assigned types:

Listing 4-3. Using types for fields

```
class MyClass {
    private myField: number;

    constructor(myField: number) {
        this.myField = myField;
    }
}
```

You can also use shorthand notation to define fields directly in the constructor parameters – the preceding snippet is functionally identical to the following:

Listing 4-4. Using a typed parameter property instead of a field to reduce code and therefore potential errors

```
class MyClass {
    constructor(private myField: number) {
    }
}
```

This shorthand creates a myField field with the same name as the parameter and assigns its value for you. Less coding and fewer bugs. These are called **parameter properties**.

Fields and parameter properties can be assigned access modifiers to change their exposure:

Listing 4-5. Access modifiers on fields and parameter properties

```
// Longhand access modifiers on fields
class MyClass {
    private privateField: number;
    protected protectedField: number;
    public publicField: number;

    constructor(
        privateField: number,
        protectedField: number,
        publicField: number,
    ) {
        this.privateField = privateField;
        this.protectedField = protectedField;
        this.publicField = publicField;
    }
}

// Same but using parameter properties shorthand notation
class MyClass {
    constructor(
        private privateField: number,
        protected protectedField: number,
        public publicField: number,
    ) {
    }
}
```

Using the shorthand notation is handy to prevent fields missing initialization; but if you *do* need to use fields, you should enable TypeScript's **strictPropertyInitialization** flag in your **tsconfig. json** file. Enabling this flag will ensure TypeScript has checked you have initialized all fields in the constructor or declared them as optional or definite properties. This affects getters and setters as well. Without this flag set, you can get situations such as the following:

Listing 4-6. Access modifiers on fields and parameter properties

```
class MyClass {
    public publicField: number;

    // As with publicField above, TypeScript allows us to
    // define this field as 'number' even though we won't have
    // initialized it until the constructor is called...
    public anotherPublicField: number;

    constructor(
        publicField: number,
    ) {
        this.publicField = publicField;
        // ...but whoops we've forgotten to initialize it! So...
    }
}

const x = new MyClass(100);
// ...when we use the field, TypeScript thinks it is a number
//    but actually it is undefined 😟😟
const y = x.anotherPublicField; // error: the value is actually
                                // undefined
                                // fix: enable
                                // 'strictPropertyInitialization'
```

Getters and Setters

Getters and **setters** allow you to define computed properties that can be accessed and modified like regular fields. The getter returns the value of the backing field, and the setter modifies it. Here's an example:

Listing 4-7. Using types on property getters and setters

```
class MyClass {
    private _myField: number;

    get myField(): number {
      return this._myField;
    }

    set myField(value: number) {
      this._myField = value * 2;
    }

    constructor(value: number) {
        this.myField = value;   // Calls 'set myField(value)'
    }
}

const x = new MyClass(10);
console.log(x.myField); // Outputs: 20
x.myField = 3;
console.log(x.myField); // Outputs: 6
```

Note that in the preceding code, we're using an underscore prefix to differentiate the field and the getter/setter internally, as otherwise we'll get a naming conflict.

Methods

Methods are functions that belong to a class instance and therefore can access the fields and other methods assigned to that instance. You can define them using the same syntax as regular functions, but without the function keyword prefix; and unless you specify an access modifier, methods default to being public.

Listing 4-8. Using types on method parameters and return types

```
class Person {
    constructor(public name: string) {
    }

    greet(another: Person): string {
        return `Hello ${another.name}, my name is
        ${this.name}!`
    }
}

const bob = new Person('Bob');
const tilly = new Person('Tilly');
tilly.greet(bob); // returns 'Hello Bob, my name is Tilly!'
```

Inheritance

Inheritance allows you to create a subclass that inherits from a parent class (a.k.a. superclass) and is performed using the **extends** keyword on the subclass. As to whether you'd actually *want* to inherit from something, we discuss in Chapter 3, in the "Structural Typing" section ☺; but if you do need to use inheritance, then subclass constructors, *if specified*, must explicitly call the superclass's constructor, and so TypeScript will check this for you if necessary:

Listing 4-9. Type safety in class inheritance

```
class Animal {
    constructor(
        private name: string,
        private sound: string
    ) {
    }

    makeSound(): void {
        console.log(`${this.name} is making a ${this.sound}
        sound`);
    }
}

class Dog extends Animal {
    constructor(name: string) {
        // When inheriting, TypeScript ensures we call the
        // parent constructor
        super(name, 'barking'); ✔
    }
}

const bugsy = new Dog('Bugsy');
bugsy.makeSound(); // Prints 'Bugsy is making a barking sound'
```

You can also use the **abstract** keyword to define **abstract classes** and **abstract methods**. An abstract class cannot be instantiated directly but can be used as a base class for other classes. An abstract method does not have an implementation and must be implemented by any non-abstract subclasses – a bit like a placeholder, if you like:

Listing 4-10. Type safety when using abstract classes

```
abstract class Shape {
    abstract getArea(): number;
}

class Square extends Shape {
    private sideLength: number;

    constructor(sideLength: number) {
        super();
        this.sideLength = sideLength;
    }

    getArea(): number {
        return this.sideLength * this.sideLength;
    }
}

const square = new Square(10);
console.log(square.getArea()); // Prints '100'
```

Implements

Interfaces allow you to define contracts for classes and other types. You can use the implements keyword to indicate that a class implements an interface. Here's an example:

Listing 4-11. Constraining a class to satisfy a TypeScript type by using the implements keyword

```
interface Printable {
    print(): void;
}
```

```
class MyClass implements Printable {
    print(): void {
        console.log('Printing...');
    }
}
```

Implementing multiple interfaces in TypeScript is simple. You just separate the interfaces with commas in the implements clause:

Listing 4-12. Implementing several interfaces

```
interface Printable {
    print(): void;
}

interface Loggable {
    log(): void;
}

class MyClass implements Printable, Loggable {
    print(): void {
        console.log('Printing...');
    }

    log(): void {
        console.log('Logging...');
    }
}
```

You can also use inheritance and implement interfaces at the same time, as in the following snippet:

Listing 4-13. Using inheritance (runtime) and interfaces (compile-time) in the same class

```
interface Printable {
    print(value: string): void;
}

class ConsoleLogger {
    log(value: string): void {
        console.log(value);
    }
    protected sanitize(value: string): string {
        // etc
    }
}

class MyClass extends ConsoleLogger implements Printable {
    constructor(private printer: Printer) {
        super();
    }
    print(value: string): void {
        // Call the superclass's 'sanitize' method
        const sanitizedValue = super.sanitize(value);
        // Print the sanitized version
        this.printer.print(sanitizedValue);
    }
}
```

Static Modifier

Fields, getters, setters, and methods can also be made static by marking them with the **static** keyword. Static members belong to the class itself, not to its instances. You can access static fields using the class name, both internally and externally.

Listing 4-14. Static getters, setters, and methods

```
class MyClass {
    private static _internalField: string = '';
    static get value() {
        return MyClass._internalField;
    }
    static set value(value: string) {
        MyClass._internalField = value;
    }
    static getFormattedValue() {
        return MyClass.value.toUpperCase();
    }
}

MyClass.value = 'hi there';
console.log(MyClass.getFormattedValue()); // Prints 'HI THERE'
```

You might have noticed that constructors cannot be static. This is because constructors return or populate the "this" binding of the class, which static members cannot access. If you want to have complex logic during initialization of a static field, you can call a static method or external function instead:

Listing 4-15. Static functions can act like static constructors

```
class MyClass {
    private static getInitialInternalClockValue(): Date {
        return new Date();
    }

    // Here we use the static method (or could be an external
    // function) to initialize the field value.
    private static _internalClock: Date =
        MyClass.getInitialInternalClockValue();

    public static get Value() {
        return MyClass._internalClock;
    }
}
```

Warning 1: Classes Are Not Types

It's important to note that while classes can be used as types in TypeScript, they are not actually the same thing as types. The difference is that classes are *values that can be instantiated* while types describe the *shape of values*. In fact, when you use a class as a type in TypeScript, the underlying language effectively translates the class into an *inline type,* names it the same as your class, and then checks incoming data against the inline type's shape, rather than against your class. This means that the following is valid in TypeScript:

Listing 4-16. Classes are computed as their type contract rather than instance during type assertions.

```
class Human {
    constructor (public name: string) {}
}

function employ(person: Human): Employee {
    return new Employee(human.name, createEmployeeNumber());
}

class Dog {
    constructor (public name: string) {}
}

const somehowWeveEmployedADog = employ(new Dog('Spot')); ✔☹
```

In the preceding example, although our **employ** function ostensibly takes a Human as its input, actually TypeScript translates the **Human** class into a *type*, so the method internally looks more like this:

Listing 4-17. Showing how the Human example type is computed as an inline type contract rather than class instance

```
function employ(person: { name: string }): Employee {
    return new Employee(human.name, createEmployeeNumber());
}
```

Therefore, any item that fulfills the minimum contract given by the type can be passed in – be it a dog, a boat, or your favorite type of dessert!

Figure 4-1. *Oops, we just granted employment to a blancmange!*

With this in mind, you *can* either start coding extra defensively:

Listing 4-18. Defensive coding

```
function employ(person: { name: string }): Employee {
    if (!(person instanceof Human)) {
        throw new Error(`Person must be of type 'Human'.`)
    }
    return new Employee(human.name, createEmployeeNumber());
}
```

or you can start embracing the functional paradigm more fully. More on this in the following section.

Warning 2: Classes Can Cause Scope Bleed

The other major problem with classes is not unique to structurally typed languages but instead is intrinsic to classes themselves. And it is the problem of scope bleed. Take the following code for example:

Listing 4-19. A simple example class

```
class Human {
    constructor (public name: string, public dateOfBirth:
    Date) { }

    age(): number {
        return new Date(
            new Date().valueOf() -
            this.dateOfBirth.valueOf()
        ).getUTCFullYear() - 1970;
    }
}
```

Seems fine right? But consider this: the **age** method has access to the **name** field. Coming from an object-oriented programming point of view, we might simply shrug at this – what does it matter? But I put it to you that we only do so because OO doesn't allow us to change this – it just happens automatically.

However, let's look at this more critically. In contrast to the aforementioned, we would balk if we saw someone submit the following code in a PR:

Listing 4-20. Demonstration of what data a calculateAge method could read or write within its scope

```
function calculateAge(name: string, dateOfBirth: Date) {
    // What is the ^^^^ name parameter doing here?? It's
    // not needed?
    return new Date(
        new Date().valueOf() -
        dateOfBirth.valueOf()
    ).getUTCFullYear() - 1970;
}
```

And, likewise, we might frown if we saw this:

Listing 4-21. Demonstration of what data a greet method could read or write within its scope

```
function greet(name: string, dateOfBirth: Date) {
    // ☺ Why pass dateOfBirth ^^^ into our greet function?
    // Seems unnecessary
    return `Hello ${name}!`;
}
```

The truth is that everything using the **this** parameter has access to *everything* shared within the class. And this chuck-everything-into-a-massive-scope-available-to-all-methods approach gets pretty tricky to test accurately the more fields and methods we add, because shared state now means the sequence you call the methods *could* impact test results and add n^x permutations.

So classes are, in practice, little bundles of mini global scopes and associated statefulness that can be very difficult to test without knowing in detail the code inside each method and how it impacts the scope and state. This means that with classes, we somewhat couple the test implementation to the class implementation, and you need knowledge of both.

As a critical approach to this, I would recommend stepping back from classes where possible and instead separating out behavior and data. Consider making data immutable, passed explicitly through parameters instead of ambiently available via mini global scopes; encapsulate behavior in stateless functions and data in behaviorless types – and essentially embrace a functional programming approach; and you will find this structural language paradigm much easier to scale and maintain.

So although in this chapter we've covered how to use classes in TypeScript, including fields, modifiers, methods, inheritance, and more, and while classes can be a useful tool in object-oriented programming, it's important to remember that they are not the only solution and may not be the best fit for all situations. In many cases, I would recommend **not using classes**, as without careful use, they can lead to the problems discussed, used within this functional, structurally typed language. Instead prefer a functional separation of immutable data and pure functions, and you'll find life easier.

Not fully convinced yet? Our next chapter will look at the amazing power that comes from instead separating data from behaviors, by allowing inline types and computed types. See you there!

Summary

In this chapter, we delved into the core concepts of classes in TypeScript, a fundamental feature of object-oriented programming (OOP). We learned how to create classes using the class keyword and how to use constructors to initialize class instances with specific data. Access modifiers played a crucial role in controlling the visibility and accessibility of class members, fields held the state of class instances, getters and setters allowed us to create computed properties and modify class fields securely, and methods enabled us to perform various operations within the class, accessing internal fields and other methods as needed.

We also covered inheritance, a core principle of OOP, allowing us to create subclasses inheriting properties and behaviors from a parent class. We learned how to use the **extends** keyword to create subclasses and how to call the parent class's constructor correctly. Abstract classes and abstract methods provided a way to define placeholders in base classes, ensuring that subclasses implemented these methods to fulfill the contract; and interfaces allowed us to define contracts for classes and other types, enabling type checking and code consistency.

However, with classes now fully understood, we also reviewed the limitations of classes in TypeScript, with an eye on the difference between classes and types. While classes can be used as types, they are not the same, and using classes as types may lead to unexpected behavior. Furthermore, we explored the problem of scope bleed in classes and how it can hinder testability and maintenance.

As we conclude this chapter, it's crucial to remember that classes are just one tool in the TypeScript toolbox. They are an important feature, essential for containing mutable state; but depending on the use case, more functional programming techniques that support JavaScript's powerful structural type features can actually prove more flexible, testable, and maintainable. By understanding the strengths and limitations of each approach, you can make informed decisions in your TypeScript projects and write code that is both effective and efficient.

These are grand claims for a paradigm. And so in the next chapter, we'll explore structural types more deeply, looking at the power of separating data from behavior through inline types and structural computed types, and see how this can be an important design step for many use cases. In short, you now understand enough of the basics – it's time to dig deeper into a powerful way to build maintainable, high-velocity systems!

CHAPTER 5

Computed Types

Introduction

Now that we have a deeper appreciation of the fundamentals of TypeScript and how it works with the dynamic structurally typed language of JavaScript, we are ready for the real fun to start! In this chapter, we will explore a powerful feature of dynamic structural typing that is supported by TypeScript, called computed types. These advanced types take advantage of the runtime-typed approach of ECMAScript and JavaScript, making TypeScript's types even more dynamic and flexible than most statically typed languages, and are one of the paradigm's most powerful features.

In TypeScript, we know a "type" is the minimum contract or shape of a value, and we have already discussed various types like booleans, strings, interfaces, etc. Now, by applying pointers or "aliases" to these, we can reference parts or computations of types and use these to construct new types. In this chapter, we will explore how type aliases can be used in a range of these ways.

One we will cover is union types. These are powerful types in functional programming languages, allowing us to guard against invalid state. We will learn how to use union types effectively to ensure the correct representation of data and restrict inputs to only valid options.

© Ben Beattie-Hood 2023

B. Beattie-Hood, *Modern TypeScript*, https://doi.org/10.1007/978-1-4842-9723-0_5

Another is intersection types, which allow us to mash types together. These help us reduce code duplication and aid reuse, allowing us to break down our structural types into atomic pieces of responsibility that can be merged and combined as needed.

A third is conditional types, which enable us to compute types based on certain conditions or patterns. These powerful types allow us to use **extends** and **infer** keywords to pattern-match against types and extract pieces of those types for further use. And we will combine these conditional types with mapped and recursive types, creating dependent correlatives that are context-aware and adaptive to input types.

Lastly, we will discover template literals in TypeScript, which allow us to embed type expressions within strings. We'll look at string transformations using these expressions, as well as how they can also be used in conditional pattern matching.

By the end of this chapter, you will have a deeper understanding of the most powerful aspect of structural types: computed types. And you'll be able to master their application in TypeScript, enabling you to create more dynamic, reusable, and expressive type definitions in your projects. So get started, and explore the amazing power of computed types!

Type Aliases

All the shapes we've discussed so far – booleans, strings, interfaces, the in-memory structural contract computed from a class, and dates – are **types**. As discussed, a "type" is what we call the minimum contract or shape of a value. And in TypeScript, because of the runtime-typed approach of ECMAScript and JavaScript, we have some additional features to types that make them even more powerful than most other statically typed languages. We'll explore these in this section on computed types.

These computed types are made possible by a powerful feature called **type aliases**. We create type aliases using the **type** keyword, like this:

Listing 5-1. Using type aliases

```
interface Person {
    name: string
    address: {
        street: string
        postcode: string
    }
}

// You can assign a type name to an in-built type...
type Email = string;
type URL = string;

// ...assign a type name to another type...
type Friend = Person;

// ...and even reuse a piece of another type...
type Address = Person['address'];
>    type Address = {
         street: string;
         postcode: string;
     }

// ...including system types!
type ArrayLength = Array<number>['length'];
>    type ArrayLength = number;

type CharAtDelegate = String['charAt'];
>    type CharAtDelegate = (pos: number) => string;
```

One way to think of type aliases is as pointers, very similar to how variables in code are pointers to values in memory. In the preceding example code, you can visualize the **Email**, **URL**, **Friend**, and **Address** type aliases as shown in Figure 5-1.

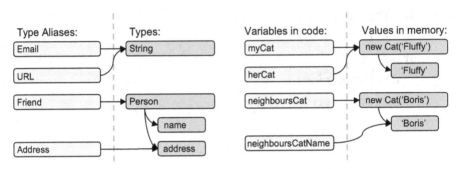

Figure 5-1. *Type aliases are like variables in code, which instead point to types rather than values*

Why would we need this? There are three use cases:

- Type aliases can give **domain-specific detail** to an otherwise nondescript type (e.g., using "Employee" instead of Person in the preceding example).

- Type aliases can act as references for **anonymous types**.

- Type aliases allow us to **reuse** a piece of a type (including recursively).

The first one is obvious and stylistic – and it's your preference if you want to use it. The other two we need to rewind and dig in a bit more to understand the real power.

Using Type Aliases

Unlike most other languages, interfaces in TypeScript can also be anonymous, with no name. How does this work? Have a look at the "page" variable in the following snippet, which has an unnamed interface defined inline:

Listing 5-2. An explicit, but anonymous, type

```
const page: { height: number, width: number } =
getCurrentPage();
```

Assigning the type to the page variable allows us to assert that the variable is being assigned the right shape of value. But defining it anonymously, inline, means we don't clutter our scope with a lot of single-use interface definitions for specific use cases.

The same goes for function args. In the function signature in the following snippet, the interface for the "args" param is unnamed and, as with the **page** type in the preceding code snippet, is declared inline:

Listing 5-3. An anonymous type used for a function parameter

```
function renderControl(args: { text: string, width: number }) {
    // ...
}
```

This ability to use unnamed types is important, because it means that we can infer, refer to, and reuse pieces of types:

Listing 5-4. Using a type alias to point to an otherwise anonymous piece of a type

```
interface Person {
    name: string
    address: {
```

```
        street: string
        postcode: string
    }
}
// Example 1: Extract a piece of a type...
type Address = Person['address'];

// ...and reuse it for a constant...
const address: Address = {
    street: '123 Street',
    postcode: 'ABC123'
}

// ...or reuse it within another type.
interface Building {
    label: string
    address: Address
}

// Example 2: Extract the parameters of a function...
type RenderControlArgs = Parameters<typeof renderControl>;

// ...reuse them to add type safety when constructing args...
const renderControlArgs: RenderControlArgs = [{
    text: 'Hello world!',
    width: 200
}]
// ...so that when we call the function we know it is safe.
renderControl(...renderControlArgs);
```

In this way, perhaps unlike any other language you've used, TypeScript will allow you to extract previously unnamed pieces of types via type aliases.

This has some important ramifications, which we'll explore next.

Union Types

Unlike most statically typed languages, ECMAScript and JavaScript allow variable pointers to be reassigned to values of a different type from their original value. For example, in JavaScript, you can do this:

Listing 5-5. JavaScript lets us reassign a variable to any given runtime shape.

```
// Foo is a number...
let foo = 9;

// ...but now it's a boolean...
foo = true;

// ...and now it's an object.
foo = { firstName: 'Jane', lastName: 'Scott' };
```

So how should we define the type of **foo**? Reading the preceding code snippet, we know that **foo**'s type could be a number *or* a boolean *or* an object structure. And so that is exactly how we can express it in TypeScript:

Listing 5-6. Using TypeScript to constrain the valid types using an "OR" operator

```
// Foo is a number...
let foo: number | boolean | { firstName: string, lastName: string } = 9; ✔

// ...but now it's a boolean...
foo = true; ✔ // ..and this is fine

// ...and now it's an object...
foo = { firstName: 'Jane', lastName: 'Scott' }; ✔
// ..and this is fine
```

```
// ...and we can't mistakenly assign foo to something invalid:
foo = new Date(); ✗ // Error: Date is not valid for our type
```

You can use the same for function parameters:

Listing 5-7. Using TypeScript to constrain the valid types for a function parameter using an "OR" operator

```
function log(value: string | boolean | number | Date);

log("Bonjour!"); ✔ // Allowed...
log(new Date()); ✔ // ...also allowed...
log({ firstName: 'Jane', lastName: 'Scott' }); ✗
    // ...nope, not allowed 👎
```

This or-ing of types together is called a **union type**. But union types don't have names – they are defined inline. So how do we extract it to use it elsewhere? We label it with a type alias.

Listing 5-8. Using a type alias to label an otherwise anonymous union type

```
// Assign a type alias to the union...
type LogValue = string | boolean | number | Date;

function log(value: LogValue);     // ...and then reuse it...
function print(value: LogValue);   // ...wherever you want...
function equals(a: LogValue, b: LogValue); // ...and so on...
const aLoggedValue: LogValue =     // ...etc...
```

Union types are a powerful feature of many functional programming languages – languages that primarily pass state between functions, rather than attach functions to state as objects. If you're more familiar with an object-oriented approach, you can think of them like enums but with extra data. And one of their most powerful features is that they can be used to guard against invalid state.

For example, let's say we are storing the pets owned by the kids in a school class. Some of the many options include cats, bugs, and fish (Figure 5-2).

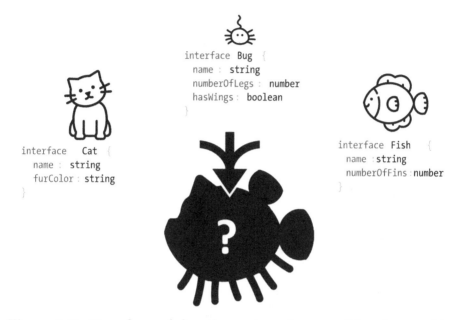

Figure 5-2. *How do we define the contract for something that could be a cat, or a bug,... or even a fish?*

Even with the flexibility of structural typing, what sort of franken-shape could be wide enough to allow all the needed options? The name field is common, but beyond that, we end up with a smorgasbord of optional fields to allow for all the valid permutations:

Listing 5-9. How should we define a type that can accept the valid data fields for the possible pet variants?

```
enum PetType {
  cat,
  fish,
  bug
}
interface Child {
  name: string
  pet: {
    type: PetType
    name: string
    furColor?: string
    numberOfLegs?: number
    hasWings?: boolean
    numberOfFins?: number
  }
}
const emma: Child = {
  name: 'emma',
  pet: {
    name: 'Boris' // oh no
  }
}
const greg: Child = {
  name: 'Greg',
  pet: {
    type: PetType.cat,
    name: 'Fuzzy',
    furColor: 'Brown',
    numberOfLegs: 7, // oh no
    numberOfFins: 3,
    hasWings: true,
  }
}
```

?

Emma's weird
unknown pet!

Greg's happy little
CatFishBug??

The problem with the enum+optional values approach is that it's easy to assign invalid data by mistake, because the enum value has no impact on the value structure.

Instead, let's try a union type, to say that only cats require fur, only bugs have wings, and only fish have fins.

Listing 5-10. Using a union type to provide structured cases for each of the pet variants

```
interface Child {
    name: string
    pet:
    | {
        name: string
        furColor: string
    }
    | {
        name: string
        numberOfLegs: number
        hasWings: boolean
    }
    | {
        name: string
        numberOfFins: number
    }
}
```

This partly solves it, as it prevents insufficient data. But it still fails because the weird **CatFishBug** unfortunately fulfills the minimum contract provided by any of the union options:

Listing 5-11. The union type allows greater type safety across dependent fields, but it is not yet perfect

```
const emma: Child = {
    name: 'emma',
    pet: {              ✗ // Nope, disallowed: not enough data 👈
        name: 'Boris'
    }
}

const greg: Child = {
    name: 'Greg',
    pet: {              ✔ // Oh no, this is still fine ☹
        name: 'Fuzzy',
        furColor: 'Brown',
        numberOfLegs: 7, // oh no
        numberOfFins: 3,
        hasWings: true,
    }
}
```

To solve it correctly, we use a literal type (remember those?) to mark the options with a required field that is unique to each case. Then TypeScript's in-place type narrowing will ensure we don't overprovide our options:

Listing 5-12. Using a literal type within our union cases allows us to distinguish them and thereby improve type safety

```
interface Child {
    name: string
    pet:
    | {
        type: 'cat'          // 🖑 Use a unique literal type to
        name: string         //    differentiate the options.
        furColor: string
    }
    | {
        type: 'bug'    // 🖑 The unique literal allows
        name: string   //    TypeScript to narrow correctly...
        numberOfLegs: number
        hasWings: boolean
    }
    | {
        type: 'fish'   // 🖑 ...saving a bunch of typos, - and
        name: string   //    preventing weird pet combinations!
        numberOfFins: number
    }
}

const emma: Child = {
    name: 'emma',
    pet: {
        type: 'cat',           ✗ // Still disallowed: not
                               // enough data 👆
        name: 'Boris'
    }
}
```

```
const greg: Child = {
    name: 'Greg',
    pet: {
        type: 'cat',
        name: 'Fuzzy',
        furColor: 'Brown',
        numberOfLegs: 7,  ✗ // Disallowed: unrecognized fields ☛
        numberOfFins: 3,
        hasWings: true,
    }
}

const tim: Child = {
    name: 'Tim',
    pet: {
        type: 'cat',  ✔ // Matches an option exactly, so allowed ☛
        name: 'Whiskers',
        furColor: 'Brown',
    }
}
```

💡 Union types are used in many of our advanced cases in
Chapter 6. See **IsEqual**, **Compute**, and **JsonOf** for examples.

Intersection Types

As we saw before, ECMAScript and JavaScript allow for a spread operator:

Listing 5-13. Using the spread operator merges two or more values together

```
const path: Path = {
    points: [[0, 0], [100, 100], [200, 100]],
    joined: true,
};

const fill: Fill = {
    color: 'blue',
};

const graphic = {
    ...path,
    ...fill,
};
```

But let's think about that in more detail for a minute: What is the type of the **graphic** variable?

In union types, we saw that we could "or" types to allow a choice of options. As shown in the preceding code snippet, the shape of the graphic variable is the combined shape of the path variable *and* the fill variable. This is called an **intersection type**, and this is how you express it in TypeScript:

Listing 5-14. TypeScript's intersection types allow us to represent the result type of two or more merged values

```
const path: Path = {
    points: [[0, 0], [100, 100], [200, 100]],
    joined: true,
};
```

```
const fill: Fill = {
    color: 'blue',
};
```

type Graphic = Path & Fill;   // Combines the two types together
```
const graphic: Graphic = {
    ...path,
    ...fill,
};
```
> *type Graphic =*
>   *interface Path {*
>   *points: [number, number][]*
>   *joined: boolean*
>   *}*
>   *&*
>   *interface Fill {*
>   *color: string*
>   *};*

We can combine intersection and union types to remix parts of types together, reducing maintenance and allowing changes to flow more easily through our type system. Let's revamp the **Child** interface to be more maintainable:

Listing 5-15. Using intersection types to reduce repetition in our union type

```
// Before:                          // After:
interface Child {                   interface Child {
  name: string                        name: string
  pet:                                pet:
  | {                                 { name: string }    // DRY 🎉
    type: 'cat'                       & (    // 🔗 Intersection type
    name: string // 👍 Repeat         | {
    furColor: string                    type: 'cat'
  }                                     furColor: string
  | {                                 }
    type: 'bug'                       | {
    name: string // 👍 Repeat           type: 'bug'
    numberOfLegs: number                numberOfLegs: number
    hasWings: boolean                   hasWings: boolean
  }                                   }
  | {                                 | {
    type: 'fish'                        type: 'fish'
    name: string // 👍 Repeat           numberOfFins: number
    numberOfFins: number              }
  }                                 )
}                                   }
```

Intersection types are a powerful way to reduce maintenance, if used to combine pieces of existing types into new types. And TypeScript comes with a range of helpful utility types for selecting pieces of types that you can combine, so we'll review these soon. But before we do, we need to get comfortable with another feature of computed types: **generics**.

💡 Explore more about intersections in the **Exclude** utility type further on in this chapter, as well as in Chapter 6's **Compute** and **UrlParameters with Optional Parameters** advanced examples.

Generic Types

Generic types are types that accept **type parameters** to modify their resulting shape. These type parameters are specified by the consuming code and act as placeholders for types – a little like type aliases, but scoped to a single type.

Type Parameters

The following example shows the use of a type parameter. The type parameter is provided (input) at the top of the type in **‹›** brackets and then can be used (output) anywhere inside the type:

Listing 5-16. Generic type parameters

```
interface List<T> {   // 👆 'T' here acts like a placeholder...
    items: T[]        // 👆 ...which we can leverage within
                      //    the type.
}
```

The type of the **items** field in the preceding code snippet's **List** object is not pre-known by the type – but using the **T** type parameter as a placeholder, we can allow the type to be specified by the consumer, like this:

Listing 5-17. Using a generic type

```
const names: List<string> = // ...
>     type List<string> = {
          items: string[];
      };

const cats: List<Cat> = // ...
>     type List<Cat> = {
          items: Cat[];
      };

const people: List<Person> = // ...
>     type List<Person> = {
          items: Person[];
      };
```

In the preceding example, we can see that the placeholders provided by the type parameters are filled in by the types passed to them when they are used.

These type parameters can be reused multiple times, anywhere within the generic type. In the following snippet, although we still don't prescribe what **T** is, we know that all instances of its use will be the same type when used:

Listing 5-18. Generic type parameters act like placeholders that assert all instances of the generic parameter match.

```
interface List<T> {
    items: readonly T[]

    addItem: (item: T) => List<T>
    removeItem: (item: T) => List<T>

    // ...etc
}
```

```
const names: List<string> = // ...etc

names.addItem('Bob');   ✓ // Works correctly
names.addItem(1234);    ✗ // Throws an error, because names has
                          // constrained its own T to enforce
                          // 'string'.

const name = names.items[0];
```
›   *const name: string;*

Generic types can also be used on functions. As in interfaces, where the type parameters allow us to tie the type of fields together, in functions, the type parameters allow us to tie function parameters and return types together without preknowledge of their specific types:

Listing 5-19. Using generic parameters in functions

```
function getFirst<T>(arr: T[], n: number): T[] {
    return arr.slice(0, n);
}

function compare<T>(a: T, b: T): number {
    return a < b ? -1 : a > b ? 1 : 0;
}
```

💡 Many examples of using generics are included in this book. See the "Utility Types" section later in this chapter for examples of generic types provided with TypeScript; or see Chapter 6 for advanced usages.

In many cases, such as with the functions in the preceding code example, it's easiest to lean on TypeScript's type inference rather than specifying the generic parameters when calling the function. This approach cuts down maintenance and boilerplate and is common practice in TypeScript:

Listing 5-20. Using generic parameters in functions

```
function compare<T>(a: T, b: T): number {
    return a < b ? -1 : a > b ? 1 : 0;
}

const firstThreeColors = getFirst(
                                🖑 TypeScript can infer the
                                   generic params
    ['Red', 'Blue', 'Green', 'Yellow', 'Purple'],
    3,
);

const sortedNames =
    ['Zoe', 'Annabel', 'Ted', 'Ross']
    .sort(compare);  🖑 TypeScript can infer the generic
    parameters
```

const Modifier on Generic Parameters

However, as discussed before, TypeScript will infer the "most useful" case for the value's types – which can lead to inferred values being less narrowly typed, reducing type safety:

Listing 5-21. Inferred generic parameters have the same default narrowness as a normal inferred type

```
function self<T>(value: T): T {
    return value;
}

const value = self({ name: 'Joan', age: 62 });
>    const value: {
        name: string;
        age: number;
    }
```

One way we've discussed persisting the literal values of the types is by marking the value **as const**, as in the following code example:

Listing 5-22. Using as const helps inferred generic parameters

```
const value = self({ name: 'Joan', age: 62 } as const);
>    const value: {
        readonly name: "Joan";
        readonly age: 62;
    }
```

This gets the needed result. But a sometimes helpful shorthand is to instead mark the generic parameter itself **as const**, as shown in the following:

Listing 5-23. Using const generic parameters reduces callsite boilerplate

```
function self<const T>(value: T): T {
    return value;
}

const value = self({ name: 'Joan', age: 62 });
```

>   *const value: {*   🖐 No **as const**
>
>   needed here! 🪡
>
>   *readonly name: "Joan";*
>
>   *readonly age: 62;*
>
>   *}*

Try this approach out if you find yourself writing **as const** too much. It is a helpful way to keep the type safety without the overhead.

Generic Constraints

Type parameters can be given constraints too. Take the following example:

Listing 5-24. A simple generic function

```
function findByName<T>(items: T[], name: string) {
    return items.find(item =>
        item.name === name  ✗ // We don't know if T has a
                                         'name' field ☹
    );
}
```

Here, we want to find the item by name – but if we don't know the type of **T**, then how do we know it has a **name** field to match on? So we add a constraint:

Listing 5-25. Constraining our function's generic parameter to require types within a subset

```
function findByName<T extends { name: string }>(items: T[],
name: string) {
    return items.find(item =>
        item.name === name
    );
}
```

This constraint means that the **T** placeholder can only be assigned a type that has our expected **name** field:

Listing 5-26. Inferred and explicit generic parameters have to meet the requirements of the constraint

```
findByName([1, 2, 3], 'Jim'); ✘ // Nope
findByName([{name:'Ava'},{name:'Jim'},{name:'Mia'}], 'Jim'); ✓
// Allowed 👍
```

These constraints act like type shapes, and so it can be tempted to use generics for more than the necessary:

Listing 5-27. Overuse of generic parameters

```
function includes<T extends { name: string }>(t: T[], name:
string): boolean {
    return t.find(item => item.name === name) !== undefined;
}
```

```
// While the above is accepted, it's simpler to write it as
// follows:
function includes(items: { name: string }[], name: string):
boolean {
    return items.find(item => item.name === name) !==
    undefined;
}
```

So a good rule of thumb with type parameters is "If a type parameter is only used once in a function signature, then you don't need a type parameter."

Inferred Type Keywords

As covered in Chapter 3, a powerful feature of TypeScript is the ability to infer the type of variables, as well as function parameters, return types, and more. The compiler can even go deep into values to compute nested types too. Here is an example:

Listing 5-28. A simple inferred type

```
const colors = {
    red: '#FF0000',
    green: '#00FF00',
    blue: '#0000FF',
} as const;
❯    const colors: {
         readonly red: "#FF0000";
         readonly green: "#00FF00";
         readonly blue: "#0000FF";
     }
```

💡 Want to revisit what we covered earlier for inferred types? You can find the earlier information in Chapter 3.

Inferred types help reduce boilerplate, sure. But what if you want to *use* that type – store it, reuse it, or manipulate it? TypeScript includes two helpful type keywords that allow you to do just this.

typeof Type Inference Keyword

The **typeof** type inference keyword allows you to reference a type inference and thereby store it in a type alias for reuse.

Listing 5-29. Storing the inferred type in a type alias

```
const colors = {
    // ...
} as const;

type Colors = typeof colors;
>    type Colors = {
         readonly red: "#FF0000";
         readonly green: "#00FF00";
         readonly blue: "#0000FF";
     }
```

As shown in the preceding example, this keyword allows us to capture the type of an existing variable, function, or object without explicitly specifying it.

This is particularly useful when we want to maintain the type information and avoid duplication. It allows us to skip writing repetitive types that are already inferable from the data:

Listing 5-30. Example of duplicated boilerplate

```
// A much more tedious alternative, formally defining the
// interface...
interface Colors {
    red: string
    green: string
    blue: string
}

// ...and then basically repeating the same code in the
// usage. 😣
const colors: Colors = {
    red: '#FF0000',
    green: '#00FF00',
    blue: '#0000FF',
};
```

Note   The **typeof** type inference keyword is unfortunately spelt exactly the same as the ECMAScript **typeof** operator that allows us to extract the primitive runtime type name of a value (see the "Runtime Assertions" section in Chapter 3). In contrast, this **typeof** type inference keyword is different from the ECMAScript operator and, like all TypeScript, is removed during the compilation to the JavaScript phase.

And of course, once you have the type, you can still do all the usual type inference and extraction you'd normally be able to do:

Listing 5-31. Reduce boilerplate by inferring the types and storing them in type aliases instead

```
const colors = {
    red: '#FF0000',
    green: '#00FF00',
    blue: '#0000FF',
};
type Colors = typeof colors;  🖼
⟩    type Colors {
         red: string
         green: string
         blue: string
     }

function greet(firstName: string, lastName: string): string;

type LastName = Parameters<typeof greet>[1];  🖼
⟩    type LastName = string;
```

keyof Type Inference Keyword

TypeScript also allows you to extract the keys of a type:

Listing 5-32. Using the keyof keyword to infer the type of a type's indexer key

```
export interface Person {
    firstName: string
    lastName: string
    age: number
}
```

```
// Extract a union of all field names within the Person type:
type KeysOfPerson = keyof Person;
>     type KeysOfPerson = "firstName" | "lastName" | "age";
```

However, if you try the following code, the type of **keys** will be **string[]**, and not a union:

Listing 5-33. Using the keyof keyword to infer the type of a type's indexer key

```
const ashley: Person = // ...define or load a person
                        // value here...

const keysOfPerson = Object.keys(ashley);
>     const keysOfPerson: string[];     // ...whaat? 😩
```

Why is this? Seems unhelpful, right?

Actually, returning **string[]** rather than **keyof** is more accurate. The fact is that while TypeScript will constrain the value matches a *minimum* of the type assigned (remember the "minimum contract" approach of structural typing?), it will not guarantee that the value only includes the fields of that type. For example, the following is valid:

Listing 5-34. Using the keyof keyword to infer the type of a type's indexer key

```
const ashley = {
    firstName: 'Ashley',
    lastName: 'Emmerson',
    age: 48,
    someAdditionalCompletelyRandomField: 42
}
```

129

```
function render(person: Person) {
    /* Enumerating over Object.keys(person) here may also
       include keys that we're not expecting. */
}
```

However, this is a much contested design approach in the TypeScript common libs – and in fact the TS libs themselves disagree by returning the strict types from the sibling **Object.values()** method. And so, if you are confident that the keys will not exceed those in the specified type, you can use an alternative strongly typed approach such as the following:

Listing 5-35. A type-safe wrapper for Object.keys

```
function keysOf<T extends Record<keyof any, any>>(x: T):
(keyof T)[] {
    return Object.keys(x);
}
```

If you prefer this approach, you may want to explore the **ts-reset** NPM package (www.npmjs.com/package/@total-typescript/ts-reset), which attempts to add stricter typing to some of the defaults shipped in TypeScript.

:Q: We use the keyof keyword in some of the types in Chapter 6. You'll find examples in the **Compute** and **JsonOf** types in that chapter.

Where's the **valueof** Type Inference Keyword?

So TypeScript provides **typeof** and **keyof** type inference operators. Why doesn't it also provide a **valueof** type inference operator?

The answer is it doesn't need to. By using type indexers (see the "Parameterized Values" section in Chapter 3), you can extract a single field's value's type, or a union of all the fields' value types:

Listing 5-36. Indexers already allow us to access the equivalent of a valueof keyword.

```
export interface Person {
    firstName: string
    lastName: string
    age: number
    dateOfBirth: Date
}

// Extract the type of a single field:
type FirstName = Person['firstName'];
>    type FirstName = string;

// Extract a union of types of all fields:
type ValuesOfPerson = Person[keyof Person];
>    type ValuesOfPerson = string | number | Date;

type PeopleArray = Person[];

// Extract a union of types of all array values:
type ValuesOfArrayItem = PeopleArray[number];
>    type ValuesOfArrayItem = Person;
```

Utility Types

TypeScript comes with a pre-built suite of utility types that you can use when constructing and intersecting your own types, to save time and maintenance. We'll be able to build our own later in this book once you get familiar with some of the more advanced concepts, but let's get a view of the most commonly used built-in ones now in this section and how we can use them.

Note   The utility types are all examples of *generic* types – when you're reviewing this section, keep in mind what we've discussed about generics and their ability to leverage **generic parameters**. As well as being important tools for constructing and managing union and intersection types, utility types will be a helpful illustration of how these generic parameters can be used.

Record<Keys, Type>

Most languages come with a dictionary or hashtable utility type, and JavaScript is no exception with its simple object, which allows developers to assign new keys and corresponding values at runtime. TypeScript comes with a built-in type called **Record<Keys, Type>** utility type that allows you to create a new type that has a set of specified properties with corresponding value types. Here's how you use it:

Listing 5-37. Using the Record<Keys, Type> utility type

```
const people: Record<string, Person> = {
    alice: { name: 'Alice', age: 30 },
    bob: { name: 'Bob', age: 35 },
};
```

This creates a type that has a **string** key and a **Person** value for each key. As it is a dictionary type and not a fixed shape, it allows key/value pairs to be added and removed from it, so long as the keys and values conform to the requirements:

Listing 5-38. Records allow us to add, update, and remove keys.

```
people['jill'] = { name: 'Jill', age: 48 };   ✓ // Allowed
delete people.alice;                           ✓ // Allowed
```

Pick<Type, Keys>

The "Pick" utility type allows you to create a new type that includes only certain properties from an existing type:

Listing 5-39. Using the Pick<Type, Keys> utility type

```
interface Person {
    name: string;
    age: number;
    address: string;
}

// Pick copies across only the specified fields:
type PersonBasicInfo = Pick<Person, 'name' | 'age'>;
❯     type PersonBasicInfo = {
          name: string;
          age: number;
      };

const alice: PersonBasicInfo =
    { name: 'Alice', age: 30 }; ✓ // Allowed
```

Let's use **Pick<Type, Keys>** a bit more practically, by making a **pick** function. Because we use a **reduce** function internally, we'll use a lambda style rather than the classic function style:

Listing 5-40. A runtime function that represents Pick<Type, Keys>

```
const pick = <T extends object, K extends keyof T>
  (t: T, ...keys: K[]): Pick<T, K> =>
    keys
    .reduce<any>(
        (result, key) => {
            result[key] = t[key];
            return result;
        },
        {},
    );
```

Now, we can use this function like so:

Listing 5-41. Using our runtime pick function

```
const fruit = {
    bananas: 'Yellow',
    kiwis: 'Green',
    watermelons: 'Pink',
} as const;

const vegetables = {
    carrots: 'Orange',
    potatoes: 'White',
    cherries: 'Red',
} as const;
```

```
const shoppingColors = {
    ...pick(fruit, 'bananas', 'watermelons'),
    ...pick(vegetables, 'carrots', 'cherries'),
};
```

> ```
>     const shoppingColors: {
>         carrots: "Orange";
>         cherries: "Red";
>         bananas: "Yellow";
>         watermelons: "Pink";
>     };
> ```

Using **Pick<Type, Keys>** in this way, we see we retain the type safety of both keys and values while keeping our code simple to read.

Omit<Type, Keys>

The **Omit<Type, Keys>** utility type allows you to create a new type that excludes certain properties from an existing type. It is the exact inverse of the **Pick<Type, Keys>** utility type. Here's the same example as shown previously, but instead using **Omit<Type, Keys>**:

Listing 5-42. Using the Omit<Type, Keys> utility type

```
interface Person {
    name: string;
    age: number;
    address: string;
}

// Omit copies across all except the specified fields:
type PersonWithoutAddress = Omit<Person, 'address'>;
```

> ```
>     type PersonBasicInfo = {
>         name: string;
> ```

```
    age: number;
  };
```

```
const alice: PersonWithoutAddress =
  { name: 'Alice', age: 30 }; ✓ // Allowed
```

However, the **Omit<Type, Keys>** utility type in TypeScript arguably has a flaw. The built-in **Pick<Type, Keys>** type ensures you only specify valid keys. In contrast, the built-in **Omit<Type, Keys>** type allows you to specify any given key without even checking if it exists in the type provided in the **Type** generic parameter. There are pros and cons to this, but usually you'll want a stricter version of this, so here is how you can build it yourself:

Listing 5-43. An alternative to the Omit type with safer types

```
type OmitStrict<Type, Keys extends keyof Type> =
  Pick<Type, Exclude<keyof Type, Keys>>;
```

Don't worry if that seems a lot to take in right now. We'll look into how this works in more detail later. For now, let's use it like we did with **Pick<Type>**, to build an **omit** function:

Listing 5-44. A runtime function that represents Omit<Type, Keys>

```
const omit = <Type extends object, Keys extends keyof Type>
  (t: Type, ...keys: Keys[]): OmitStrict<Type, Keys> =>
  Object.entries(t)
  .filter(([key]) => !keys.includes(key as Keys))
  .reduce<any>(
    (result, [key, value]) => {
      result[key] = value;
      return result;
    },
    {},
  );
```

And then let's use this like we did with the **pick** function:

Listing 5-45. Using our runtime omit function

```
const fruit = {
    bananas: 'Yellow',
    kiwis: 'Green',
    watermelons: 'Pink',
} as const;

const vegetables = {
    carrots: 'Orange',
    potatoes: 'White',
    cherries: 'Red',
} as const;

const shoppingColors = {
    ...omit(fruit, 'bananas'),
    ...omit(vegetables, 'carrots', 'cherries'),
};
❯    const shoppingColors: {
        potatoes: "White";
        kiwis: "Green";
        watermelons: "Pink";
    };
```

Notice how using **OmitStrict<Type, Keys>** (or the more loosely typed **Omit<Type, Keys>**) we again retain the type safety of both keys and values while keeping our code simple to read.

💡 We use this utility type to make a **ShallowMerge** type, when working with intersection types in Chapter 7.

Partial<Type>

The **Partial<Type>** utility type allows us to create a new type that makes all properties of an existing type optional. Using our same Person example, we can make the fields optional:

Listing 5-46. Using the Partial<Type> utility type

```
interface Person {
    name: string;
    age: number;
    address: string;
}

type PartialPerson = Partial<Person>;
>     type PartialPerson = {
          name?: string | undefined;
          age?: number | undefined;
          address?: string | undefined;
      };

const alice: PartialPerson = { name: 'Alice' }; ✓ // Allowed
```

One example of use for this is in a value setter for a store, where any fields you might assign are saved to the store:

Listing 5-47. Example usage of the Partial<Type> utility type

```
interface Store<T> {
    value: T
    setValue: (newValue: Partial<T>) => void
}

const formDataStore = createStore({
    firstName: 'Jean',
    lastName: 'Hawkes',
```

```
    age: 80,
});

// Ginny's lastName didn't change, so we don't have to include
// it in the Partial<Person> data:
formDataStore.setValue({
    firstName: 'Ginny',
    age: 81,
})
```

💡 This type is used in the "Mapped Types" section of this chapter, with code showing how it works, as well as in the **UrlParameter with Optional Parameters** type in Chapter 6.

Required<Type>

Like **Pick<Type, Keys>** and **Omit<Type, Keys>**, the built-in **Required<Type>** utility type is the handy inverse of **Partial<Type>**. Here's an example:

Listing 5-48. Using the Required<Type> utility type

```
interface Person {
    name: string;
    age?: number;
    address?: string;
}
```

```
type RequiredPerson = Required<Person>;
```
```
❯     type RequiredPerson = {
          name: string;
          age: number;          👈 // These fields now
          address: string;            // become required
      };
```
```
const bob: RequiredPerson = {   ✘ // Missing required
field: address
    name: 'Bob',
    age: 30,
};
```
```
const alice: RequiredPerson = {
    name: 'Alice',              ✓
    age: 30,                    ✓
    address: '123 Main St.',    ✓
};
```

Readonly<Type>

In TypeScript, you can preface fields with the **readonly** keyword to make
them immutable:

Listing 5-49. Marking fields readonly prevents write access

```
interface Person {
    readonly name: string;
    readonly age: string;
}
```
```
const alice: Person = { name: 'Alice', age: 30 };
```
```
alice.name = 'Dave'; ✘ // Disallowed by TS: readonly property 👈
```

However, if you want to do this for all the fields within a type, this gets cumbersome. And so the **Readonly<Type>** utility type allows you to create a new type that makes all properties of an existing type readonly and therefore cannot be changed:

Listing 5-50. Using the Readonly utility type to avoid boilerplate

```
interface Person {
    name: string; // No need to repeat the readonly
    age: number;  // keyword on every property 👆
}

type ReadonlyPerson = Readonly<Person>;
>    type ReadonlyPerson = {
         readonly name: string;
         readonly age: number;
     };

const alice: ReadonlyPerson = { name: 'Alice', age: 30 };

alice.name = 'Dave'; ✗ // Disallowed by TS: readonly
                        // property 👆
```

The **Readonly<Type>** type is therefore used as the return type of **Object.freeze(t)**, communicating to the compiler that the result of this function call cannot be mutated.

However, it's worth knowing that this type, as well as the result of **Object.freeze(t)**, is shallow. This means that although direct fields of the object cannot be edited, nested subobjects and arrays *can* still be edited, and so sometimes you will want a recursive alternative to **Readonly<Type>**, such as the following example:

Listing 5-51. A DeepReadonly type that allows us to make a deep-nested object entirely readonly

```
type DeepReadonly<T> =
    T extends (undefined | null | boolean | string | number |
    Function)
        ? T // Primitives are immutable by default.
    : T extends Array<infer U>
    // Arrays, maps & sets have special
        ? ReadonlyArray<DeepReadonly<U>>
    // built-in readonly modifier types.
    : T extends Map<infer K, infer V>
    // ...ditto
        ? ReadonlyMap<DeepReadonly<K>, DeepReadonly<V>>
    // ...ditto
    : T extends Set<infer M>
    // ...ditto
        ? ReadonlySet<DeepReadonly<T>>
    // ...ditto
    : { readonly [K in keyof T]: DeepReadonly<T[K]> };
    // 🔁 Deep recursion.
```

Don't worry about those tricky infers and ternaries yet – we'll get to these in the "Conditional Types" section, later in this book. For now, take the preceding code snippet as a handy recursive implementation that will protect even deep field values, as shown in the following:

Listing 5-52. Using our DeepReadonly utility type

```
interface Person {
    name: string;
    age: number;
    addresses: {
        street: string
        postcode: string
    }[]
}
```

const alice: **DeepReadonly\<Person>** = { name: 'Alice', age: 30, addresses: [] };

alice.addresses[0].street = '123 Some Street'; ✗
// Yay! disallowed 🎉

If you'd like to use immutable data structures in more depth, it's best to use the library "Immer".

To remove the readonly effect on a type, you can use the following utility type:

Listing 5-53. Removing the effects of readonly from a type

```
type Mutable<Type> = {
    -readonly [K in keyof Type]: Type[K]
}

type EditablePerson = Mutable<ReadonlyPerson>;
❯    type EditablePerson = {
        firstName: string;
        age: number;
    }
```

Exclude<Type, Keys>

The **Exclude<Type, Keys>** utility type creates a new type by excluding all keys that match the **Keys** parameter from the type specified by the **Type** parameter. Mainly you'll use this to reduce union types to cases you want to support, in cases similar to the following:

Listing 5-54. Using the Exclude<Type, Keys> utility type

```
type HttpMode = 'GET' | 'PUT' | 'POST' | 'DELETE'

type SupportedHttpMode = Exclude<HttpMode, 'PUT' | 'DELETE'>
>    type SupportedHttpMode = "GET" | "POST";

function httpRequest(mode: SupportedHttpMode, url: string);
httpRequest('DELETE', "/api/person"); ✗ // Disallowed
httpRequest('GET', "/api/person");    ✓ // Allowed
```

As shown, you'll probably find many uses for the **Exclude<Type, Keys>** utility type when working with unions provided by third parties. But there's another important use case for **Exclude<Type, Keys>** that you should definitely keep in your toolbelt – and it relates to solving a problem with intersection types. See the following code example:

Listing 5-55. Problems with intersection types merging props

```
interface ComponentPropsA {
    foo: string
    bar: number
}

interface ComponentPropsB {
    foo: () => void
    baz: number
}
```

144

```
type MergedComponentProps = ComponentPropsA & ComponentPropsB
```
>   *type MergedComponentProps = {*
>   *foo: string & () => void;   // 🐉 Yikes! 💀*
>   *bar: number;*
>   *baz: number;*
>   *}*

This is actually valid behavior – values in ECMAScript can be made to fulfill several types. But this is not usually what you want, because of the way that spread works:

Listing 5-56. The spread operator overwrites previous data

```
const componentPropsA = {
    foo: 'Hello',
    bar: 42
}

const componentPropsB = {
    foo: () => console.log('Hello world'),
    baz: 3
}

const mergedComponentProps = {
    ...componentPropsA,
    ...componentPropsB,   // foo here overwrites, so is a lambda
                          // not a string
}
```

Instead of using simple intersections, we can use the **Exclude<Type, Keys>** utility type to remove the overlaps before intersecting the types:

Listing 5-57. Use the exclude utility type to avoid overlapping keys

```
type ShallowMerge<A, B> = {
    [P in Exclude<keyof A, keyof B>]: A[P];
} & B;

type MergedComponentProps =
    ShallowMerge<ComponentPropsA, ComponentPropsB>
>    type MergedComponentProps = {
        foo: () => void;        // 🫰 Much better! 👍
        bar: number;
        baz: number;
    }
```

In fact, **Omit** actually uses **Exclude** internally for this very sort of thing, and so the preceding code snippet can be simplified further to the following:

Listing 5-58. A simpler version of our ShallowMerge utility type

```
type ShallowMerge<A, B> =
    Omit<A, keyof B> & B;    // 🫰 Perfect! 😄
```

So **Exclude** is an important utility type that can be used for powerful results.

💡 We use this utility when removing fields in the "Mapped Types" section of this chapter, as well as in the **JsonOf** type in Chapter 6.

Extract<Type, Keys>

As with **Pick**/**Omit** and **Partial**/**Required**, the **Extract<Type, Keys>** utility type is the invert of the **Exclude<Type, Keys>** utility type. As such, it creates a new type by excluding all types that match the **Keys** parameter from the type specified as **Type**. So you can use it as a convenience type in similar situations:

Listing 5-59. Using the Extract<Type, Keys> utility type

```
type HttpMode = 'GET' | 'PUT' | 'POST' | 'DELETE'

type SupportedHttpMode = Extract<HttpMode, 'PUT' | 'DELETE'>
>    type SupportedHttpMode = "PUT" | "DELETE";

function httpRequest(mode: SupportedHttpMode, url: string);
httpRequest('DELETE', "/api/person"); ✓ // Allowed, cp Exclude
httpRequest('GET', "/api/person");    ✗ // Disallowed,
                                           cp Exclude
```

💡 We use this utility when in the **UrlParameters** type in Chapter 6.

Parameters<FunctionType>

The **Parameters<FunctionType>** utility type extracts the parameter types of a function type and returns them as a tuple.

Listing 5-60. Using the Parameters<FunctionType> utility type

```
type MyFunctionType = (x: number, y: string) => void;

type MyFunctionParameters = Parameters<MyFunctionType>;
>    type MyFunctionParameters = [number, string];
```

This can be useful in many cases. One such case is ensuring wrapping functions match parameters without needing to code them yourself:

Listing 5-61. Using the Parameters<FunctionType> utility type more practically

```
// We don't have to update our code if the parameters of the
// fetch func are changed:
function fetchWrapper(...params: Parameters<typeof fetch>) {
    const [urlOrRequest, ...others] = params;
    console.log(urlOrRequest);
    return fetch(urlOrRequest, ...others);
}
```

Another handy use for this is gaining reference to types not directly exposed by third-party libraries that you need to use:

Listing 5-62. Reusing types via the Parameters<FunctionType> utility type

```
// In a third-party library, they've forgotten to export a handy
// interface we need, and instead only exported a function:
interface PrivateRectangleShape {
    height: number
    width: number
}

export function drawRectangle(rect: PrivateRectangleShape);

-----------------------------------------------------------------

// In our own code, to use the unexported interface, we can use
Parameters<T>:
```

```
type Rectangle = Parameters<typeof drawRectangle>[0];

const rect: Rectangle = {
    height: 5,
    width: 3,
}
```

Notice we're using the indexor **[0]** to extract the first (albeit only) parameter from the parameters tuple in this case. See the "Parameterized Values" section for more info.

ConstructorParameters<ClassType>

As with the **Parameters<FunctionType>** utility type, the **Constructor Parameters<ClassType>** utility type extracts the parameter types of a constructor function type and returns them as a tuple:

Listing 5-63. Using the ConstructorParameters<ClassType> utility type

```
class Shape {
    constructor(x: number, y: number, color: Color) {}
}

type ShapeConstructorParameters =
ConstructorParameters<typeof Shape>;
>    type ShapeConstructorParameters = [number,
number, Color];
```

ReturnType<FunctionType>

The **ReturnType<FunctionType>** utility type extracts the return type of a function type.

Listing 5-64. Using the ReturnType<FunctionType> utility type

```
// Get return type of a type...
type Greeter = (name: string) => string;
type GreeterResult = ReturnType<Greeter>;
>    type GreeterResult = string;

// ...or a function interface...
interface Validation {
    (value: any): boolean;
}
type ValidationResult = ReturnType<Validation>;
>    type ValidationResult = boolean;

// ...or an object's field/method.
interface MyShape {
    getArea: () => number;
}
type ShapeArea = ReturnType<MyShape['getArea']>;
>    type ShapeArea = number;
```

The use of **Parameters<FunctionType>** and **ReturnType<FunctionType>** utility types to alias and reuse types required by the methods on third-party libraries is a nice way to keep your code constrained without adding maintenance.

But unfortunately this doesn't work well when inferred types require generic parameters. For example, this won't compile:

Listing 5-65. Limitations of TypeScript syntax for generics

```
// This won't work:
function merge<A, B>(a: A, b: B): InternalMergedType<A, B> {
    // ...
}

type MergeResult = ReturnType<typeof merge<Foo, Bar>>;
// 🤖⚠ Compiler fail!
type MergeResult = ReturnType<typeof merge(1, 2)>;
// 🤖⚠ Compiler fail!
```

If you need to use **Parameters<FunctionType>** and **ReturnType<FunctionType>** in these cases, you need to supply the generic parameters beforehand, as in the following workaround:

Listing 5-66. Working around limitations of TypeScript syntax for generics

```
function merge<A, B>(a: A, b: B): InternalMergedType<A, B> {
    // ...
}
const wrapperToMergeFooAndBar = (foo: Foo, bar: Bar) =>
merge(foo, bar);

type MergeResult = ReturnType<typeof wrapperToMergeFooAndBar>;
// Works 👍
```

Conditional Types

From this point onward, things are going to get even more interesting. Let's look at another feature of JavaScript being a dynamic language. In the following example, what is the return type of the function?

Listing 5-67. What is the return type of a function containing conditions (e.g., if statements)?

```
function parseBoolean(s: string) /* 😝 What is the return type
here? */ {
    if (s === 'yes') {
        return true;
    }
    if (s === 'no') {
        return false;
    }
    throw new Error(`Unrecognized boolean value ${s}`);
}
```

What we want is a type that essentially represents the logic of the function in the example, like this:

1. If **s** is "yes", then the return value's type is **true**.

2. If **s** is "no", then the return value's type is **false**.

3. Otherwise, the return value's type is **never**.

The return type depends on the literal type of "s", so we need to make "s" into something we can interrogate as a type. We can do this by making it a generic parameter:

Listing 5-68. Store the subject type of the condition so that we can use it to compute the return type.

```
function parseBoolean<S extends string>(s: S) /* now we can
query 'S' */ {
    // ...
}
```

Using the generic parameter, we can use TypeScript to *encode the logic of the function* as a type ternary, called a **conditional type**. And to make this, we need to use the **extends** keyword.

extends Keyword

Knowing the logic inside the **parseBoolean** function, we can write its return type as a type ternary, or "conditional type," like this:

Listing 5-69. A simple conditional type

```
type ParseBooleanResult<S> =
    S extends 'yes' ? true
    : S extends 'no' ? false
    : never;

function parseBoolean<S extends string>(s: S):
ParseBooleanResult<S> {
    // ...
}

const a = parseBoolean('yes');
>    const a: true;
const b = parseBoolean('no');
>    const b: false;
const c = parseBoolean('carrots and bananas');
>    const c: never;
```

This special **extends** keyword ternary is the normal way to write conditional types. There is an alternative stylistic approach that we'll cover in the "Conditional Types via Property Accessors" section, further down, but for now, let's concentrate on this standard (and more powerful) approach. The **extends** keyword allows you to check if a type covers *at least* the contract specified. Here's another example:

Listing 5-70. TypeScript early-exits when evaluating conditional types.

```
interface Person {
    name: string
    email?: string
    phone?: string
    address?: {
        street: string
        postcode: string
    }
}
// Here the extends keyword allows us to do pattern-matching
// against type T.
type PrimaryContactDetails<T extends Person> =
  T extends { email: string } ? T['email']
  : T extends { phone: string } ? T['phone']
  : T extends { address: string } ? T['address']
  : never;

function getPrimaryContact<T extends Person>(p: T):
PrimaryContactDetails<T> {
    // ...
}
```

Leveraging the "minimum contract" aspect of structural typing, we can see in the preceding example how the **extends** keyword allows us to effectively achieve pattern matching against the type. Notice how the ternary, like normal ternaries in JavaScript, is early-exiting, so we only match one result even if the type could match other options:

Listing 5-71. Our conditional type in action

```
const x = getPrimaryContactDetails({
    name: 'Dave',
    email: 'dave@email.com',
    phone: '012345678',
} as const)
>    const x: "dave@email.com";
    // 🖑 The 'email' case has precedence in the type's
    ternary's ordering
```

💡 Pattern matching via the extends keyword is essential for all of our advanced cases in Chapter 6. See **IsEqual**, **JsonOf**, **Flatten**, and **UrlParameters** for examples.

`infer` Keyword

Where the **extends** keyword allows us to use pattern matching to compute type shapes, the **infer** keyword takes the pattern matching even further to give you access to the parts of the pattern you didn't match on.

Let's take an example to illustrate. Let's make a type that will give us the "head" element of an array (the first item in the array). Using pattern matching, we could do it like this:

Listing 5-72. The head of an array could be one of many different types

```
type HeadOf<T extends any[]> =
    T extends string[] ? string
    : T extends number[] ? number
    : T extends boolean[] ? boolean
    : T extends Date[] ? Date
    : T extends ... // Oh no, how many of these cases do we
                        need to write..??!
    ...etc...
    ...etc...
    ...etc...
```

But we can see in the preceding example that it would be hard to cover every case, and our pattern matching would end up unmanageably long. Instead, the **infer** keyword allows us to just pattern-match that **T** is an array and then *infer* the actual type of the array from the match:

Listing 5-73. Pattern matching in conditional types using the infer keyword to store the located type

```
type HeadOf<T extends any[]> =
    T extends (infer Head)[] ? Head
    : never;
```

Well, that was a lot simpler, wasn't it? ☺ The **infer** keyword allows us to infer and store the rest of a matched type into an inline type, which can then be used a bit like a generic parameter thereafter.

This ability to infer types is very powerful and can be used in a lot of handy ways. For example, you can infer the value of a generic parameter:

Listing 5-74. Inferring the type of a generic parameter

```
type HeadOf<T> =
    T extends Iterable<infer Head> ? Head
    : never;

// Now our HeadOf<..> type works with non-arrays too:

const a: HeadOf<NodeList> = // ...
>    const a: Node;

const b: HeadOf<Set<string>> = //...
>    const b: string;

const c: HeadOf<Map<string, Person> = //...
>    const c: [string, Person];
```

You can also infer function parameters:

Listing 5-75. Inferring the type of a function's parameters

```
type ParametersOf<T> =
    T extends (...params: infer Params) => any ? Params
    : never;
// ...or even a function's returned type:
type ReturnOf<T> =
    T extends () => infer Returned ? Returned
    : never;

// (This is how TypeScript's inbuilt Parameters<T> and
// ReturnType<T> utility types work)
```

```
const params: ParametersOf<typeof console.log> = // ...
```
>   *const params: [message?: any, ...optionalParams: any[]];*

```
const interval: ReturnOf<typeof window.setInterval> = // ...
```
>   *const interval: number;*

And lastly you can pattern-match on tuples and infer their contents:

Listing 5-76. Inferring the types of a tuple's values

```
type MixItUp<T> =
    T extends []
        ? []
    : T extends [infer First]
        ? [First]
    : T extends [infer First, infer Last]
        ? [Last, First]              // 😄
    : T extends [infer First, ...infer Middle, infer Last]
        ? [...Middle, First, Last]   // 🤯!
    : never;

const a: MixItUp<[1]> = // ...
```
>   *const a: [1];*

```
const b: MixItUp<[1, 2]> = // ...
```
>   *const b: [2, 1];*

```
const c: MixItUp<[1, 2, 3, 4, 5, 6, 7]> = // ...
```
>   *const c: [2, 3, 4, 5, 6, 1, 7];*

Extracting Inferred Types

There are cases where it is useful to use the infer keyword outside of a conditional type. You can use the following technique for this:

Listing 5-77. Returning an inferred type allows us to assign it to a type alias and therefore reuse it

```
interface WrappedType<T> {
    id: number
    name: string
    description: string
    value: T
}

type Unwrapper<W extends WrappedType<any>> =
    W extends WrappedType<infer T>
        ? T        ↩ // Effectively return the inferred type
        : never;

type PackagedPerson = WrappedType<Person>;
type ExtractedPerson = Unwrapper<PackagedPerson>;
❯    type ExtractedPerson = Person; // the extracted
                                    // inferred type
```

In fact, this is actually how utility types like React's **ComponentProps<C>** type work:

Listing 5-78. React's ComponentProps<C> utility function works by returning the inferred generic parameter

```
type ButtonProps = React.ComponentProps<typeof Button>;
```

159

If you need more than one type returned, you can return them as an inline type instead:

Listing 5-79. Returning more than one inferred type

```
interface WrappedType<A, B, C> {
    a: SomeComplexType<A>
    b: SomeComplexType<B>
    c: SomeComplexType<C>
}

type Unwrapper<W extends WrappedType<any, any, any>> =
    W extends WrappedType<infer A, infer B, infer C>
        ? {
            a: A
            b: B
            c: C
        }
        : never;

type ReshapedType<W extends WrappedType<any, any, any>> =
    SomeNewType<
        Unwrapper<W>['a'], ↩ // Use the inferred types
        Unwrapper<W>['b']     // provided by the Unwrapper's
                              // inline return type.

    >
```

The preceding method can also be improved by using the advanced caching technique detailed in the "Inline Caching Using Conditional Types" section in Chapter 7.

Distributive and Nondistributive Conditional Types

One quirk of conditional types is that if you assign a union type to any of the generic parameters, the conditional type is applied to *each member of the union type*. This is called a **distributed conditional type**, because the conditional is distributed across the union.

Listing 5-80. Each case of a union is matched against a conditional type, and the result re-unioned as a "distributed conditional type"

```
type ArrayOf<T> =
    T extends any ? T[]
    : never;

// Given...
type A = ArrayOf<string | number>;
// ...TS's conditional typing is 'distributed' onto each member
// of the union, therefore the above becomes equivalent to...
type A = ArrayOf<string> | ArrayOf<number>;
// ...whose individual conditional types then evaluate down to
// essentially:
type A = string[] | number[];
```

The reason TypeScript uses this "distributing" behavior on unions is because the aforementioned is the outcome most usually needed. However, in some cases, this isn't helpful – take the following example:

Listing 5-81. Example of when conditional unions' distributive behavior isn't desired

```
// We want A = { items: (Cat | Dog)[] }
type CatsAndDogs = List<Cat | Dog>

// But distribution means that the above evaluates to...
type A = List<Cat> | List<Dog>

// ...which is essentially this:
type A = { items: Cat[] } | { items: Dog[] }    😵‍💫
```

Not helpful if you want to store both, right? Well, there's a neat trick we can use to make unions nondistributive, which is to wrap the generic in a tuple during comparison – which circumvents TypeScript's default behavior:

Listing 5-82. Method for avoiding distributive unions in conditional types if necessary

```
type List<T> =
    [T] extends any[] ? { items: T[] }    🙎
    : never;

type A = List<Cat | Dog> // 🎉 equivalent to A = { items: (Cat
| Dog)[] }
```

Conditional Types via Property Accessors

In some cases, where your conditional type is only comparing a type to literal type values, you may use a stylistic alternative as shown in the following code snippet:

Listing 5-83. Using a type indexer as an alternative to conditional type

```
// Longhand conditional type:
type HexOfColor<Color extends string> =
    Color extends 'Red' ? '#ff0000'
    : Color extends 'Green' ? '#00ff00'
    : Color extends 'Blue' ? '#0000ff'
    : Color extends 'White' ? '#ffffff'
    : Color extends 'Black' ? '#000000'
    : never;

// VS a conditional type alternative via property accessor:
interface ColorNameToHexMap {
    Red: '#ff0000'
    Green: '#00ff00'
    Blue: '#0000ff'
    White: '#ffffff'
    Black: '#000000'
}
type HexOfColor<Color extends keyof ColorNameToHexMap> =
ColorNameToHexMap[Color];

const green: HexOfColor<"Green"> = '#000000'; ✗ // Error
const green: HexOfColor<"Green"> = '#00ff00'; ✓ // Correct
```

Mapped Types

Conditional types, as we've just looked at, are a form of what are called computed types – types that compute a target type from a source type. In conditional types, we've seen how to perform a simple wholesale translation of source to result type. In **mapped types**, we can perform a more granular transformation by translating each individual field in the source type.

Changing the Type of Fields

To translate individual fields in a type, we need to use a tool we've looked at previously: type indexes. The following example is a quick refresher:

Listing 5-84. A simple dictionary

```
type StringStringDictionary = {
    [key: string]: string
}

const favouriteThings: StringStringDictionary = {};
>    const favouriteThings: {
         [key: string]: string;
     };

favouriteThings['color'] = 'Red';
```

If we couple this with Ok, fine – but we've covered indexed types. How do they help us transform? Well, let's refine the indexed type we have to take a generic parameter:

Listing 5-85. Adjusting the index to match the keys of the type supplied via the generic parameter

```
type OurType<T extends object> = {
    [Key in keyof T]: string
}
```

This is now a mapped type – it has exactly the same fields as the type specified in the generic parameter, but redefines (maps) the field values to new types, in this case strings. Let's see how this works in a more practical example:

Listing 5-86. Creating a simple mapped type

```
interface Person {
    firstName: string
    lastName: string
}

type OurType<T extends object> = {
    [Key in keyof T]: boolean
}

const validatedPersonData: OurType<Person> = {} as any;

validatedPersonData['firstName'] = true;      ✓
validatedPersonData['lastName'] = false;      ✓
validatedPersonData['color'] = true;          ✗  // Invalid key
validatedPersonData['lastName'] = 'Foo';      ✗
// Invalid value
```

Great – now we've constrained the key to match the key of a generic type parameter. But we're still not exactly *transforming* the type – how do we do that?

Now that we have constrained the index key, we can use that index key as a field reference to reference each field, as follows:

Listing 5-87. Mapping our field values to the types in the originating type supplied via our generic parameter

```
type OurType<T extends object> = {
    [Key in keyof T]: T[Key]
}
```

The preceding simplistic example would match every field of the computed type the same type as the originating field – so firstName would be string, age would be number, etc.

Now, let's bring in other computational types to translate each field loosening the fields by unions to make them (for example) nullable or optional:

Listing 5-88. Extending the field values in our mapped type to also permit null

```
// Transforming (mapping) the type: Changing the type of each field
// in this case to also allow null.
type Nullable<T extends object> = {
    [Key in keyof T]: T[Key] | null 👆
}
const doug: OurType<Person> = {
    firstName: 'Doug',    ✓ // All fields now allow values per their
    lastName: null,       ✓ // originating type, OR null, to be
                            // assigned.
    age: 'Ten',           ✗ // But we can't assign incorrect
                            // type values,
    aage: 5,              ✗ // nor make typos.
}
```

```
type Partial<T extends object> = {
    [Key in keyof T]?: T[Key] // Shorthand, equivalent to
                              // 'T[Key] | undefined'
}                       👆
const someOfDoug: Partial<Person> = {
    firstName: 'Doug',
    lastName: 'Smith',
        // Remaining fields are acceptable now to leave as
        // 'undefined'
}

// The inverse of Partial uses an adjustment in the special
// syntax to remove the undefined as a valid value for the field.
type Required<T extends object> = {
    [Key in keyof T]-?: T[Key]
}                       👆 Shorthand to make non-optional
                           (prohibiting undefined)
```

...or extending the fields using generics:

Listing 5-89. Extending the field values in our mapped type to be history metadata

```
interface Person {
    name: string
    age: number
    dateOfBirth: Date
}

interface HistoryEntry<T> {
    value: T
    effectiveDate: Date
}
```

167

```
type History<T> = {
    [Key in keyof T]: HistoryEntry<T[Key]>[]
}

type Result = History<Person>;
    >    type Result = {
            name: {
                value: string
                effectiveDate: Date
            }[];
            age: {
                value: number
                effectiveDate: Date
            }[];
            dateOfBirth: {
                value: Date
                effectiveDate: Date
            }[];
        }
```

...or using conditional types to translate the field values themselves:

Listing 5-90. Using conditional types to adjust the field values'
types on a case-by-case basis

```
interface Person {
    name: string
    age: number
    dateOfBirth: Date
}

type TypesOf<T extends object> = {
    [Key in keyof T]:
        T[Key] extends boolean ? 'I am a boolean'
```

```
            : T[Key] extends number ? 'I am a number'
            : T[Key] extends Date ? 'I am a date'
            : T[Key] extends string ? 'I am a string'
            : never;
}

type Result = TypesOf<Person>
>    type Result = {
         name: "I am a string";
         age: "I am a number";
         dateOfBirth: "I am a date";
     }
```

Adding and Removing Fields

Adding fields to a mapped type is simple – we can add new fields by using an intersection:

Listing 5-91. Adding fields to a type by using an intersection type

```
// Add new fields by using an intersection:
type WithEmployeeData<T> = {
    employeeNumber: string
    startedDate: Date
} & T;

// Now TS requires the employee fields to be defined too:
const doug: WithEmployeeData<Person> = {
    firstName: 'Doug',
    lastName: 'Smith',
    age: 21,
    employeeNumber: '12345',
    startedDate: new Date(2000, 1, 1)
}
```

💡 You can also use the **ShallowMerge** utility type from Chapter 7 as a safer alternative than direct type intersection when adding fields.

But how can we remove fields? As seen before, we can use the **Exclude<T, U>** utility type to remove values from a union. **keyof T** is a union, so we can use **Exclude<T, U>** to remove keys from it:

Listing 5-92. Removing a field by excluding it from the type

```
type Remove<T, RemoveKey extends keyof T> = {
    [Key in Exclude<keyof T, RemoveKey>]: T[Key]
};

function remove<T, RemoveKey extends keyof T>(value: T, key:
RemoveKey): Remove<T, RemoveKey> {
    const result = { ...value };
    delete result[key];
    return result;
}

interface Employee {
    name: string
    employeeNumber: string
    favoriteColor: string
}
const bob = {
    name: 'Bob Smith',
    employeeNumber: 'A01234',
    favoriteColor: 'Purple',
} satisfies Employee;
```

```
const redacted = remove(bob, 'name');
```
> *const redacted: {*
>   *employeeNumber: string;*
>   *favoriteColor: string;*
> *}*

Renaming Fields

As well as adding and removing fields, you can also use mapped types to rename fields. To do this, you use the **as** keyword to cast the field key to a new type. The following code example shows the cleanest way of doing this, by casting to a generic type that can do the renaming for us. This example makes use of conditional types that we've already covered, as well as template literals that are covered later in this chapter:

Listing 5-93. Renaming fields using a template literal

```
interface Person {
    firstName: string
    lastName: string
    age: number
}

type RenamedField<Key extends keyof any> =
    Key extends string ? `${Key}_renamed` : Key;

type Rename<T> = {
    [Key in keyof T as RenamedField<Key>]: T[Key]
}

// Rename all fields
type Result = Rename<Person>;
```
> *type Result = {*
>   *firstName_renamed: string;*

```
        lastName__renamed: string;
        age__renamed: number;
    }
```

🔆 We cover **template literal types** later in this chapter.

Recursive Types

As well as mapping over the contents of a type, you can also map recursively into a type, using type recursion. We will explore two ways of doing this: recursion within an object type and recursion over a tuple type.

Recursion Within an Object Type

To recurse within an object type, we use the same index over the **keyof T** approach; but we also recursively call our own mapped type for field types as needed:

Listing 5-94. An example recursive type

```
type SaveData<T> = {
    id: number
    value: T
    dateSaved: Date
}
```

```
type Saved<T extends object> = SaveData<{
    [Key in keyof T]:
        T[Key] extends object
            ? Saved<T[Key]>    ☞    // Recursion into subfields
                                    // as needed
            : T[Key]
}>

interface Person {
    firstName: string
    lastName: string
    address: {
        street: string
    }
}

type SavedPerson = Saved<Person>;
  ❯     type SavedPerson = {
          id: number;
          value: {
              firstName: string;
              lastName: string;
              address: {
                  id: number;
                  value: {
                      street: string;
                  };
                  dateSaved: Date;
              };
          };
          dateSaved: Date;
      }
```

🔆 See this technique used in more detail in Chapter 6, in the **JsonOf** and **UrlParameters** examples.

Recursion over a Tuple Type

To recurse over a tuple type, you use a conditional type to extract each value from the tuple and map it and then pass the remainder to a recursive call as follows:

Listing 5-95. Using conditional types and the rest operator to recurse through a tuple type

```
type MapValue<T> =
    T extends ...etc   🔹 // Fill this out with your own
                           // mapping conditional

// Then use it to map the recursively evaluated item types from
the tuple:
type MapTuple<T extends readonly any[]> =
    T extends readonly [infer Item]
        ? readonly [MapValue<Item>]
    : T extends readonly [infer Item, ...infer Rest]
        ? readonly [MapValue<Item>, ...MapTuple<Rest>]
    : never;
```

Why would we do this? When you are dealing only with an array, it's easy to change the type as shown in the following code:

Listing 5-96. Returning a simple array result, we lose any narrowness of the input value.

```
type SaveData<T> = {
    id: number
    value: T
    dateSaved: Date
}

// T[] goes in, SaveData<T>[] comes out. But is this all
// we need?
function save<T>(values: T[]): SaveData<T>[] {
    return values.map((value, id) =>
        ({ id, value, dateSaved: new Date() }));
}
```

However, using simple arrays gives a less safe developer experience when the number of items could otherwise be knowable:

Listing 5-97. Without the narrowness translated to the save method's return type, we lose some type safety.

```
const people = ['Kelly', 'Jim', 'Ash', 'Fiona'] as const;

const fiona = people[700]; ✗ // TypeScript knows there are
                            // only 4 items in this tuple,
                            // so helpfully flags this error.

const savedPeople = save(people);     // Returning a simple
                                      // array means
❭    const savedPeople: SaveData<string>[];
                    // TypeScript no longer knows the result is
                    // still 4 items long...
```

```
const savedFiona = savedPeople[700];    // ...and so where is
                                        // should flag an
>    const savedFiona: SaveData<string> // error, instead it
                                        // assumes the
                                        // value exists 🐞
```

So instead we can map the returned tuple type to preserve the const type data:

Listing 5-98. Without the narrowness translated to the save method's return type, we lose some type safety.

```
// Use of readonly array below supports the tuple 'as const'
shorthand.
type Result<T extends readonly any[]> =
    T extends readonly [infer Item]
        ? readonly [SaveData<Item>]
    : T extends readonly [infer Item, ...infer Rest]
        ? readonly [SaveData<Item>, ...SaveResult<Rest>]
    : never;

function save<Values extends readonly any[]>(values: Values):
Result<Values> {
    return values.map(value => ({ value, dateSaved: new Date()
    })) as any;
}

const people = ['Kelly', 'Jim', 'Ash', 'Fiona'] as const;
```

```
// TypeScript now infers savedPeople to be a correctly-typed
// tuple with the right number of elements:
const savedPeople = save(people);
```
>   *const savedPeople: readonly [*
>   *SaveData<"Kelly">,*
>   *SaveData<"Jim">,*
>   *SaveData<"Ash">,*
>   *SaveData<"Fiona">*
>   *];*

```
// And so it will correctly flag if we index erroneously:
const savedFiona = savedPeople[700]; ✗
```

```
// And will be able to correctly infer derived or subvalues:
const fiona = savedPeople[3].value;
```
>   *const fiona: "Fiona"; ✓*

💡 Dig deeper into this technique in Chapter 6, in the **Flatten** type.

Template Literals

Template literals allow you to embed type expressions within string literals. To define a template literal, use backticks "`` ` ``" rather than simple quotes around your string literal, as shown in the following example:

Listing 5-99. Defining a template literal type

```
type Email = `${string}@${string}.com`;

const wrong1: Email = 'Porridge';      ✗
const wrong2: Email = 'steve@example'; ✗
const correct: Email = 'steve@example.com'; ✓
```

As these template literals can include any type that can be evaluated to a string, you can include union types in them:

Listing 5-100. Using a union type in a template literal

```
type DomainSuffix = 'com' | 'org' | 'net';

type Email = `${string}@${string}.${DomainSuffix}`;

const wrong: Email = 'steve@example.toast'; ✗
const correct: Email = 'steve@example.com'; ✓
```

TypeScript also includes some special string-translation utility types for use with string types, which of course can be used with template literals:

Uppercase<StringType>	Changes the given string type to its uppercase equivalent
Lowercase<StringType>	Changes the given string type to its lowercase equivalent
Capitalize<StringType>	Changes only the first character in the given string type to its uppercase equivalent
Uncapitalize<StringType>	Changes only the first character in the given string type to its lowercase equivalent

Template literals can also be used in conditional types, and the embedded templated types inferred, as shown here:

Listing 5-101. Matching against a template literal in a conditional type and capturing pieces of matched string as new types

```
type SystemCaseFullname<Name extends string> =
    Name extends `${infer FirstName} ${infer LastName}`
        ? `${Capitalize<FirstName>} ${Uppercase<LastName>}`
        : Capitalize<Name>;
```

```
function toSystemCase<Name extends string>(n: Name):
SystemCaseFullname<Name>;

const name = toSystemCase('jane smith');
❯    const name: "Jane SMITH";
```

Summary

In this chapter, we explored the amazing concept of "computed types" in TypeScript, which leverages the runtime-typed approach of ECMAScript and JavaScript to make TypeScript's type system even more powerful and flexible. This will be a new concept to many, and don't worry if this chapter needs revisiting a few times while you get to grips with this idea.

To recap, in this chapter, we began with understanding type aliases, which act as pointers to types, or pieces of types. Type aliases enable us to write cleaner and more maintainable code by allowing us to reuse types rather than duplicating them. And in this chapter, we used these type aliases to provide pointers to our computed types, which would otherwise be anonymous.

Then the first computed type we reviewed was union types, which are essential for guarding against invalid states. These union types allow us to constrain only to the valid options and help us enforce specific requirements for each option.

Intersection types were the next computed type we explored, which allowed us to combine multiple types into new types, reducing code duplication and allowing us to instead design types around single responsibilities – picking and merging them as needed and reducing our ongoing type definitions overall.

We reviewed generic types, which allow us to create flexible and reusable code by accepting type parameters. We saw how generic types can be used like placeholders or algebraic parameters on functions and interfaces, enabling us to tie different parts of a type together without prior knowledge of their specific types.

We then looked at some additional keywords for inferred types, **typeof** and **keyof**, which allow us to extract types from values whose type we don't already have. And we reviewed the utility types built into TypeScript's default library, which provide useful shortcuts for common type operations. Further utility types can be found in the "Further Reading" section in Chapter 6.

Armed with unions, intersections, generics, and type extraction – collectively the scissors and glue of type DIY – conditional types took us even further into the realm of dynamic typing. We saw how, by using the **extends** and **infer** keywords, we could perform pattern matching and type inference and transform types based on specific conditions.

We then used these conditional types to create mapped types including recursive types. These powerful transformations across whole objects or arrays allow us to convert type inputs into correlative outputs, persisting the action of an operation in the translated return result.

And we finished off by looking at template literals, which let us embed type expressions within string literals. This allowed us to match and infer against pieces of strings and manipulate these into computed result types too.

By now mastering these computed types, you now have a powerful set of tools at your disposal to create sophisticated translative type definitions in TypeScript. These allow you to persist types across function calls, translating input types into result types. This allows you to use more inferred types across your system as well as keep a stricter type check on your code, and so as you continue your journey through TypeScript, you will find that computed types play a crucial role in maintaining low friction and error-resistant code bases. Happy coding!

CHAPTER 6

Advanced Usage

Introduction

By this chapter, you will have covered now all the types needed to build truly amazing software. In this chapter, we will use the types you've learned and combine them to solve advanced use cases, as a form of master class in TypeScript. For each type I will present, we will review the needs of the type, consider what types we have in our toolbelt that can address these needs, and then combine and build our advanced types step-by-step from the ground up together, so you can see how they're built and how to make the choices necessary when practicing TypeScript at an advanced proficiency.

We will start with the simpler of these advanced type challenges and use these to create types that in turn can be used to validate stages in the latter advanced types. And in finishing, I'll also list some places for further exploration of advanced types that can help you continue your learning journey and connect you to communities that can help you as you progress.

Now, on to the first advanced case!

© Ben Beattie-Hood 2023
B. Beattie-Hood, *Modern TypeScript*, https://doi.org/10.1007/978-1-4842-9723-0_6

Expect and IsEqual

To create this type, we will use

- Generics
- Union types
- Pattern matching
- Deferred types

If you've written runtime tests before, you'll be familiar with assertion libraries. The Mocha test framework uses the Chai assertion library; others such as Jest and Playwright use built-in assertion libraries. These provide the **equals** function you can use to assert that a value matches your expectations. So as we'll be building the types in this section from ground up, let's start by making our own *compile-time* assertion library, to make it faster to test our types!

What we want is a type we can use like this:

Listing 6-1. Our desired IsEqual type

```
type OurType<U> = {
    // Fancy TypeScript here to (eg.) convert a union into
    // an array
}

type IntendedResult = [1, 2, 3];

type Result = IsEqual<OurType<1 | 2 | 3>, IntendedResult> ✓
type Result = IsEqual<number, IntendedResult> ✗
```

Unfortunately, the most straightforward conditional here will not work:

Listing 6-2. A simple, but incomplete, approach to the IsEqual type

```
type IsEqual<A, B extends A> = A;

// It works!
type Result = IsEqual<1, 1>; ✓

// It works!
type Result = IsEqual<1 | 2 | 3, "Invalid value">; ✗

// It doesn't work ☹
type Result = IsEqual<1 | 2 | 3, 1>; ✓
```

The problem is that in that last type, we want **IsEqual** to assert that the first and second arguments are equal types, not just that **B** is compatible with **A**. To solve this, break it into two parts: equality and then assertion.

The equality part is tricky. We can't use a simple conditional like the following because that'll do the same thing – only compare compatibility:

Listing 6-3. The problem with our simple approach

```
type IsEqual<A, B> =
    A extends B
        ? true
        : false;

type Result = IsEqual<1 | 2 | 3, 1>;
>    type Result = true; ☹
```

We're going to need to go a bit deeper here. To solve this, we're going to use a feature of how conditional operators are implemented internally in TypeScript (this is the *Advanced* Usage chapter, alright?): conditional types allow you to compare **extends** against generic functions and types; but to allow this, they would need to be able to compare the type parameters of the generics too, and these generic parameters are unknown so they cannot be compared. Instead, conditional operators internally *defer* the match and require the generic parameters and related types of both branches match each other directly. And this *direct match* is what we want to leverage for our **IsEqual** type. The result is this:

Listing 6-4. Using deferred types to match cases exactly, rather than matching via extension

```
type IsEqual<A, B> =
    (<T>() => T extends A ? 1 : 2) extends
        (<T>() => T extends B ? 1 : 2)
// 1. ^ T is unknown, so extends requires it ^ is identical to
//    this param.
// 2. And because it is identical, extends instead resolves
//    both sides down to be *f(A) extends f(B)* - which it
//    assumes can only be true if both X and Y are the
//    -same- value.
        ? true
        : false;
```

Great! Now we have a type that checks types are equal. Now, we can use a type constraint to surface the true/false result:

Listing 6-5. Converting our true/false result type into a testable assertion for types

```
type Assert<T extends true> = T;

type ResultN =
    Assert<IsEqual<1 | 3 | 3, 1>>; ✘ // Yay, it works!
type ResultY = Assert<IsEqual<1, 1>>;   ✔ // Yay, it still works!
```

184

This has limitations – it won't work in *some* intersectional type cases. In most cases, this won't matter too much; but if it does, you'll need to go further than this chapter should cover, and you should use the extended implementation from the NPM type-plus package (`www.npmjs.com/package/type-plus`) to do this detailed type comparison. Further than this, if you are interested in a more full-featured test library for types, you may find Misha Kaletsky's `https://github.com/mmkal/expect-type` interesting to review.

Compute

 To create this type, we will use

- Generics
- **keyof** type inference
- Union types
- Mapped types
- Intersection flattening

When you make a computed type in TypeScript, it will display the type as shown in Figure 6-1.

```
interface Employee {
    employeeNumber: number
    startDate: Date
}

interface Person {
    firstName: string
    lastName: string
    address: Address
}

interface Address {
    street: string
}
                type EmployedPerson = Employee & Person
type EmployedPerson = Employee & Person;
```

Figure 6-1. *TypeScript doesn't always show the most useful type*

While accurate (and fast), this output is not very enlightening! ☺ So our next type will be a type that instead displays the actual fields of a computed type, so we can see what's going on.

To do this, let's use a mapped type, to get all the fields from a target type defined in our generic parameters, and then pull all the fields onto our own type.

Listing 6-6. Copying the keys from a complex type (e.g., intersection) onto a new type in order to simplify them

```
// For every key available across the whole of T, assign it
// to the same field's type (essentially copying type T into
// ourselves).
type Compute<T> = {
    [Key in keyof T]:
        T[Key]
};
```

```
type EmployedPerson = Compute<Employee & Person>;
>    type EmployedPerson = {
         employeeNumber: number;
         startDate: Date;
         firstName: string;
         lastName: string;
         address: Address;
     }
```

Great! But nested types (e.g., **address** field) are still obscured. To solve this, we can use a recursive intersection type to force computation of all the fields, as follows:

Listing 6-7. Adding recursion for nested objects and arrays

```
// We sort our unions by most-likely case first to allow TS to
// execute faster where possible.
type Primitive =
    | string
    | number
    | null
    | undefined
    | boolean
    | bigint
    | symbol;

type Compute<T> = {
    [Key in keyof T]:
        T[Key] extends Primitive | Date
            ? T[Key]
            : Compute<T[Key]>
};
```

However, in practice, this does exactly the same thing (Figure 6-2).

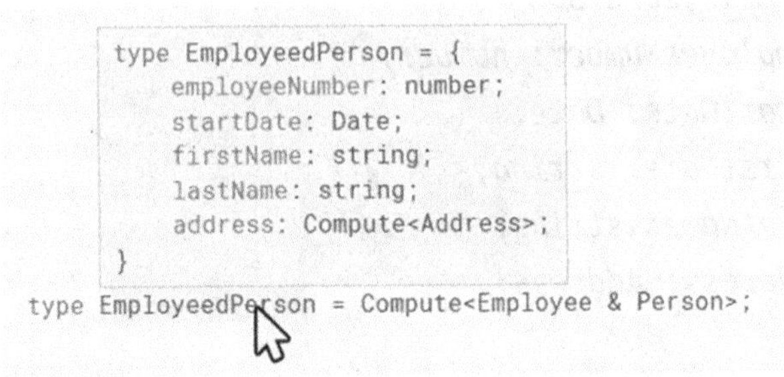

Figure 6-2. *Our Compute type shows us more helpful information*

What we need is to force TypeScript to *process* all the fields, and not take any shortcuts. One way to do this is to use an intersection type (**&**) – as discussed before, TypeScript merges all the fields from an intersection rather than overriding them, and to do this, it has to process them. We don't need to intersect to add any new fields, so we just intersect against a known empty type – the easiest built-in one being the **unknown** type:

Listing 6-8. Intersecting triggers exact computation of all keys

```
type Compute<T> = {
    [Key in keyof T]:
        T[Key] extends Primitive | Date
            ? T[Key]
            : Compute<T[Key]>
} & unknown;

type EmployeedPerson = Compute<Employee & Person>;
>    type EmployeedPerson = {
        employeeNumber: number;
        startDate: Date;
        firstName: string;
        lastName: string;
```

```
      address: {
          street: string;
      };
  }
```

JsonOf

To create this type, we will use

- Generics
- Mapped types
- Conditional types
- Recursive types
- Union types
- **keyof** type inference
- Pattern matching
- Union type stripping

Let's now use some more of our computed types to build the return type for this function:

Listing 6-9. Our target use case for a JsonOf<T> utility type

```
function toPlainJsonObject<Value>(value: Value): ??? {
    return JSON.parse(JSON.stringify(value));
}
```

We will start with an example:

Listing 6-10. Demonstrating the need for a type-safe approach to JSON.parse

```
interface Person {
    id: number
    name: string
    dateOfBirth: Date
    address: {
        street: string
        postcode: string
        movedInOn: Date
    }
}

const jenny = {
    id: 1,
    name: 'Jenny',
    dateOfBirth: new Date(1990, 1, 1),
    address: {
        street: '123 Some Street',
        postcode: '1234',
        movedInOn: new Date(2020, 1, 1),
    },
} satisfies Person;

const result = toPlainJsonObject(jenny);
>    const result = any;    ⮌  // ☹ We can do better than this
```

It would be more helpful if the function had returned a result type more like this:

Listing 6-11. An example of the mapping we'd need in the result

```
type JsonOf<Person> = {
    id: number
    name: string
    dateOfBirth: string
    address: {
        street: string
        postcode: string
        movedInOn: string
    }
}
```

For JSON, we convert the following:

From	To
boolean	boolean
number	number
string	string
Date	string

So our result type is a mapped type of **Value**, with a conditional field type that translates following the aforementioned mappings:

Listing 6-12. Mapping the fields to their serialized forms

```
type JsonOf<T extends object> = {
    [Key in keyof T]:
        T[Key] extends boolean | number | string ? T[Key]
        : T[Key] extends Date ? string
        : never
}
```

But this isn't quite right:

Listing 6-13. Don't forget nested types!

```
type Result = JsonOf<Person>;
>    type Result = {
           id: number;              ✓ // Yay, it worked!
           name: string;            ✓ // Yay, it worked!
           dateOfBirth: string;     ✓
           address: {               ✗ // Oh no, we forgot
               street: string;      ✓ // nested objects
               postcode: string;    ✓
               movedInOn: Date;     ✗
           };
     }
```

So we need to recurse into the child value, like so:

Listing 6-14. Adding recursion for nested types

```
type JsonOf<T extends object> = {
    [Key in keyof T]:
        T[Key] extends string | number | boolean ? T[Key]
        : T[Key] extends Date ? string
        : T[Key] extends object ? JsonOf<T[Key]>
        : never
}
type Result = JsonOf<Person>;
>    type Result = {
           id: number;          ✓
           name: string;        ✓
           dateOfBirth: string; ✓
```

```
    address: {                    ✓
        street: string;           ✓
        postcode: string;   ✓
        movedInOn: Date;    ✓ // Yay, it worked!
    };
}
```

But thinking more about it, why not allow JsonOf to be used on more than object types, as in practice, strings, numbers, objects, and arrays, all can be converted to JSON. So finally, let's invert our mapped type so that the conditional is topmost:

Listing 6-15. Supporting recursion over arrays

```
type JsonOf<T> =
    T extends string | number | boolean ? T
    : T extends Date | symbol ? string
    : T extends object ? {
        [Key in keyof T]: JsonOf<T[Key]>
    }
    : T extends (infer Item)[] ? JsonOf<Item>
    : never;

type A = JsonOf<string>;    ✓
type B = JsonOf<number>;    ✓
type C = JsonOf<Person>;    ✓
type D = JsonOf<Person[]>; ✓
```

One last step to take now – when converting to JSON, all function values are set to **null** in arrays and are removed from objects. Setting to null is easy, but excluding functions is more tricky and needs a couple of utility types. Let's do that next:

Listing 6-16. Excluding fields that are function types

```
// Utility type 1: Map the keys to their values, but may any
// key whose value is of type ExcludeValues to never
type ExtractKeysNotMatching<T extends object,
ExcludeValues> = {
    [Key in keyof T]: T[Key] extends ExcludeValues ?
    never : Key
}

interface Test {
    foo: string
    bar: number
    baz: () => {}
}

type Result1 = ExtractKeysNotMatching<Test, () => {}>
>      type Result1 = {
           foo: "foo";
           bar: "bar";
           baz: never;  🖎
               // Mapped to never, now we need to exclude it
       }
```

```
// Utility type 2: Get all field value types of T as a union
// (any never values are excluded by TypeScript, because you
// can't have a union against never)
type ValuesAsUnion<T extends object> = T[keyof T];

type Result2 = ValuesAsUnion<
    ExtractKeysNotMatching<Test, () => {}>>
```
>   *type Result2 = "foo" | "bar"*

Great! Now we have a way to exclude functions. Let's put the whole thing together:

Listing 6-17. The final code for our JsonOf type

```
type ExtractKeysNotMatching<T extends object,
ExcludeValues> = {
    [Key in keyof T]: T[Key] extends ExcludeValues ?
    never : Key
}

type ValuesAsUnion<T extends object> = T[keyof T];

type JsonOf<T> =
    T extends string | number | boolean ? T
    : T extends Date | symbol ? string
    : T extends Function ? null
    : T extends object ? {
        [Key in ValuesAsUnion<
                ExtractKeysNotMatching<T, () => {}>
            >]: JsonOf<T[Key]>
    }
    : T extends (infer Item)[] ? JsonOf<Item>
    : never;
```

Flatten

  To create this type, we will use

- Generics

- Tuple types

- Recursive types

- Pattern matching

In our next advanced type, we want to represent the return type of the following function:

Listing 6-18. Our target use case for our Flatten type

```
function fullFlatten<Values extends unknown[]>(values:
Values): ??? {
    const result: unknown[] = [];
    function visit(x: unknown) {
        if (Array.isArray(x)) {
            x.forEach(visit);
        }
        else {
            result.push(x)
        }
    }
    values.forEach(visit);
    return result;
}

const flattenedArray = fullFlatten([1, 2, [3, [4], 5], 6])
>    const flattenedArray = [ 1, 2, 3, 4, 5, 6 ]
```

The current built-in return type for **Array.flat()** loses the result order for tuples, so we can also improve on this.

As a start, we know from the "Recursive Types" section in Chapter 5 that in order to transform an array or tuple, we need to deal with one item at a time – by inferring the first (or "head") element of the array, transforming it, and then passing the remainder of the array into a recursion of our own type. So we can start by writing the skeleton of our type like this:

Listing 6-19. Using conditional types' pattern matching allows us to infer the types of the head and remaining elements.

```
type Flatten<T extends unknown[]> =
    T extends [infer Head, ...infer Rest]
        ? // Do something
        : [];
```

Next, we know that we need to check if the head element is an array. If it is, then we need to instead call **Flatten** on it too and then spread that into our result array; otherwise, we can just add the value directly to our result array. Either way, this done, we can then recurse on the rest of the input array, as shown in the following code:

Listing 6-20. Recursively flatten the head element, and then repeat for the remaining elements.

```
type Flatten<T extends unknown[]> =
    T extends [infer Head, ...infer Rest]
        ? Head extends unknown[]        // Is the head element
                                        // an array?
            ? [
                ...Flatten<Head>,       // if so, flatten it &
                                        // include it
```

197

```
            ...Flatten<Rest>,        // (and then continue);
    ]
    : [
        Head,                        // otherwise, just
                                     // include it
        ...Flatten<Rest>,            // (and then continue)
    ]
  : [];
type Result = Flatten<[1, 2, [3, [4], 5], 6]>;
>    type Result: [ 1, 2, 3, 4, 5, 6 ];
```

UrlParameters

To create this type, we will use

- Generics
- Tuple types
- Type recursion
- Type indexes
- Template literals
- Pattern matching
- Utility types

For this type, we want to provide the parameter type for the following method:

Listing 6-21. Our target use case for our UrlParameters type

```
function interpolateUrl<Url extends string>(url: Url,
parameters: ???) {
    // ...
}

const result = interpolateUrl(
    'api/person/:personId/address/:addressId',
    {
// Here we want our function to type-check the arguments needed
// against the given Url.
        personId: '123',   ✓
        addressId: '1',    ✓
        doesNotExist: 'foo'✗
    }
);
>   const result = 'api/person/123/address/1';
```

To do this, we need to construct a record type for the parameters whose keys are dictated by the **:param** patterns in the URL string.

We can split up a URL string into parts using recursion across the string, matching it against template literals to extract pieces of the URL as types:

Listing 6-22. Using a conditional type, we can infer the pieces of the template literal and then use them to construct the result.

```
type SplitUrl<Url> =
    // If Url is a string containing at least one '/', then
    // infer anything
```

199

```
// before the first '/' as Head, and anything after it as
// Rest, a bit like with a tuple:
Url extends `${infer Head}/${infer Rest}` ? [Head,
...SplitUrl<Rest>]

// Otherwise, if Url is a string (therefore without a '/'),
// then use it directly:
: Url extends string ? [Url]

// Otherwise, we cannot split up the type.
: never;
```

```
type Result = SplitUrl<'api/person/:personId/address/:addressId'>;
>    type Result = ["api", "person", ":personId", "address",
     ":addressId"]
```

Now, we can convert the result tuple into a union using an index or and then use **Extract** (the utility type, the opposite of **Exclude**) to get just those keys that match another string template type:

Listing 6-23. Filter the extracted pieces of the URL pattern to only those matching the pattern we're using for URL parameters.

```
type Result = SplitUrl<'api/person/:personId/address/:addressId'
>[number];
>    type Result = "api" | "person" | ":personId" | "address" |
     ":addressId"
```

```
type Result =
    Extract<
        SplitUrl<'api/person/:personId/address/:addressId'>
        [number],
        `:${string}`
    >;
>    type Result = ":personId" | ":addressId"
```

Now we just construct a record with that type:

Listing 6-24. Our final result is a record using the keys we extracted for the URL parameters

```
function interpolateUrl<const Url extends string>(
    url: Url,
    parameters: Record<Extract<SplitUrl<Url>[number],
    `:${string}`>, string>
) {
    // ...
}
```

UrlParameters with Optional Params

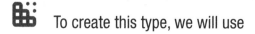 To create this type, we will use

- Generics
- Tuple types
- Type recursion
- Type indexes
- Template literals
- Pattern matching
- Utility types
- Intersection types
- Multitype inference

Let's improve our UrlParameters example to allow for optional parameters too, as shown in the following code example:

Listing 6-25. Example how we could specify optional URL parameters

```
const result = interpolateUrl(
    'api/person/:personId/(address/:addressId)',
    {
        personId: '123',
        // addressId not specified, as it is optional
    }
);
const result = 'api/person/123/';
```

The type for parameters is now more like this:

Listing 6-26. Our improved UrlParameters type: a combination of required and optional parameters

```
type Result =
    Record<RequiredParameters, string>
    & Partial<Record<OptionalParamters, string>>;

>    type Result = {
        personId: string
        addressId?: string
    }
```

So now we need to split up our string into two groups of results. To do this, we return an object with known fields – one an array of required fields and the other an array of optional fields:

Listing 6-27. Collecting the required and the optional fields into separate fields of a result type

```
type SplitUrlWithOptionals<Url> =
    // We match for the '(abc/xyz)/Rest' template before its
    // non-optional counterpart, as elsewise our match will
    // assume that the () are part of the required
    // parameter names:
    Url extends `(${infer Head})/${infer Rest}`
        ? (
            {
                required: []
                optional: SplitUrl<Head>
            }
            & SplitUrlWithOptionals<Rest>
        )
    // Again, match for the '(abc/xyz)' template before its
    // non-optional counterpart:
    : Url extends `(${infer Head})`
        ? {
            required: []
            optional: SplitUrl<Head>
        }
    : Url extends `${infer Head}/${infer Rest}`
        ? (
            {
                required: SplitUrl<Head>
                optional: []
            }
```

```
            & SplitUrlWithOptionals<Rest>
    )
  : Url extends string
      ? {
            required: [Url]
            optional: []
      }
  : never;
```

Unfortunately, this won't work. The intersections will end up trying to intersect subtypes such as the following, which we cannot index to extract a value for (it will index to return **never** because a value could not fulfill both variants):

Listing 6-28. The problem: non-intersecting fields are merged to a never type

```
type ComputedIntersection = {
    required: ['a'],
    optional: ['b'],
} & {
    required: ['y'],
    optional: ['z']
}

type Result = ComputedIntersection['required'][number];
>     type Result = never; ☹☹
```

Instead, we need to merge the subtypes instead of intersecting them, merging together the values in each array:

Listing 6-29. Merging the array fields instead of intersecting them

```
type MergeUrlParamSplits<A extends {
    required: unknown[]
    optional: unknown[]
},
B extends {
    required: unknown[]
    optional: unknown[]
}> = {
    required: [...A['required'], ...B['required']]
    optional: [...A['optional'], ...B['optional']]
}

type SplitUrlWithOptionals<Url> =
    Url extends `(${infer Head})/${infer Rest}`
        // Instead of intersections, we deep-merge the results
        ? MergeUrlParamSplits<
            {
                required: []
                optional: SplitUrl<Head>
            },
            SplitUrlWithOptionals<Rest>
        >
    : Url extends `(${infer Head})`
        ? {
            required: []
            optional: SplitUrl<Head>
        }
    : Url extends `${infer Head}/${infer Rest}`
        // (here too):
        ? MergeUrlParamSplits<
```

```
        {
            required: SplitUrl<Head>
            optional: []
        },
        SplitUrlWithOptionals<Rest>
    >
: Url extends string
    ? {
        required: [Url]
        optional: []
      }
: never;

type Result =
    SplitUrlWithOptionals<
        "user/:userId/(dashboard/:dashboardId)/(:another)"
    >;
>   type Result = {
        required: ["user", ":userId"];
        optional: ["dashboard", ":dashboardId", ":another"];
    }
```

That's looking better. Now we apply the same technique with the
Extract utility type.

Listing 6-30. Applying our same Extract filter to include only the
URL parameters

```
type UrlData =
    SplitUrlWithOptionals<"api/person/:personId/
    (address/:addressId)">;
```

```
type Result =
    Record<Extract<UrlData['required'][number],
`:${string}`>, string>
 & Partial<Record<Extract<UrlData['optional'][number],
`:${string}`>, string>>
>    type P = {
        ":personId": string;
        ":addressId"?: string | undefined;
    }
```

Nearly there. Now we reduce the **Record<Extract<...>>** repetition and rewrite the keys to strip the leading '**:**' using a mapped helper type, and we're done:

Listing 6-31. Our final version, making Record<Extract<...>> into a reusable type and cleaning up the field names at the same time

```
type RecordOfUrlParams<UrlParams extends string> = {
    [UrlParam in Extract<UrlParams, `:${string}`> as
        // 💬 rewrite the keys to remove the leading ':'s
        UrlParam extends `:${infer Param}` ? Param : never
    ]: string;
}

type UrlParamsOf<T extends string> =
    RecordOfUrlParams<SplitUrlWithOptionals<T>['required']
    [number]>
    & Partial<RecordOfUrlParams<SplitUrlWithOptionals<T>
    ['optional'][number]>>

// Let's test it out:
type Result = UrlParamsOf<'api/person/:personId/
(address/:addressId)'>
```

```
>    type Result = {
         personId: string;
         addressId?: string | undefined;
     }
```

```
// & here's our original function again, but using our improved
// UrlParamsOf:
function interpolateUrl<const Url extends string>(
    url: Url,
    params: UrlParamsOf<Url>
): string {
    // ...
}

const url = interpolateUrl(
    'api/person/:personId/(address/:addressId)',
    { "personId": '123' }                   ✓   // Type
    safety 🐢
)
```

Further Reading

To explore more advanced type construction, several libraries that are worth exploring in this area are as follows:

- HOTScript (www.npmjs.com/package/hotscript)

- type-plus (www.npmjs.com/package/type-plus)

- type-fest (www.npmjs.com/package/type-fest)

- ts-toolbelt (www.npmjs.com/package/ts-toolbelt)

There are also libraries more actively leveraging tooling such as described in this chapter: validation libraries such Zod and others, runtime libraries like Civet (`https://civet.dev/`), and functional libraries like Ramda (`https://ramdajs.com/`) all have great examples of these techniques in use.

The aforementioned libraries also have communities – smaller for the newer ones, but quite large for established ones like ts-toolbelt – that are also worth connecting with as you progress in your TypeScript learning. Through getting stuck in and contributing to projects like these, you'll develop a deeper appreciation of the design and a fuller understanding of the "why?" behind the decisions that go into these libraries, and you'll be able to modify and steer their direction as you gain more mastery in TypeScript and in package design. There's nothing like working in a team to help accelerate your learning and improve your skills.

Summary

Congratulations! By completing this chapter, you have mastered the use of the full range of TypeScript's type system. In walking through these step-by-step advanced type tutorials, you have drawn from a powerful toolbox of types and combined the results understandingly into your desired outcomes. Now, equipped with this knowledge, you will be able to create truly amazing results!

We started off this chapter with the **IsEqual<A, B>** utility type, which allowed us to perform compile-time assertions similar to runtime tests. By leveraging union types, pattern matching, and deferred types, we successfully built a type that checks for exact type equality, providing a valuable tool for the rest of this chapter and for your continued exploration of TypeScript types.

Next, we built the **Compute<T>** utility type, which provided a more readable version of any complex type in TypeScript. We used mapped types and leaned on a trick with intersections to flatten the value of **T** into a simpler shape. The result is a useful tool for debugging and reviewing your code when you are building your own advanced types.

We then stepped through the **JsonOf<T>** type, which enabled us to translate TypeScript types into their JSON equivalents. Translating each field of a mapped type through a conditional type and recursing into nested objects gave us the skeleton; then using union type stripping to remove function fields, we found our ideal result. The final version allows us to cope with all kinds of scenarios and provides a powerful tool for working with JSON-like structures in TypeScript.

By building a **Flatten** utility type next, we recursed and flattened tuples with nested elements into a strictly typed flat tuple result. This time we needed tuple type constraints to ensure we could sequence through the type accurately, recursive types to step through the elements, and pattern matching to get the value of each element in the tuple. The final type was a fully flattening generic, which we can use for a more predictable and consistent return type when flattening complex arrays.

Finally, we delved into the **UrlParameters<Url>** type, which offered type safety for interpolating parameters into URLs. We used template literals to pattern-match against parts of the input URL; and then as with the **Flatten** type, we used tuple types and recursion to map across these parts and map them into a union. This union we then used as a key for a **Record<T, string>** utility type to give our result.

Not satisfied there, we developed the **UrlParameters<Url>** type even further then to also cater for a syntax for optional parameters. We used similar techniques to before, but in parallel, and then used multitype inference to extract out both the required and optional sets of parameters, turn these into keys, and enjoy our final result. The final utility type here may be useful in the future for URL-building cases; but much more so it is an exercise of all we have covered in this book and a good check for ourselves to know that we really have now mastered TypeScript types – from beginning to end.

As you now continue your TypeScript journey, I again encourage you to engage with the communities, exploring the advanced type construction, and through them discover more libraries and tools that can enhance your TypeScript development experience.

By mastering these advanced types and utilities, you have taken significant strides in becoming a TypeScript expert. These tools will empower you to write more maintainable, reliable, and expressive code, ultimately making you a more effective TypeScript developer. I hope this chapter has expanded your horizons and prepared you to face even more complex type challenges with success!

CHAPTER 7

Performance

Introduction

We have mastered the language; now we must master the tool. As helpful as TypeScript is, it also represents a step between writing your code and running it in production. Large or complex code bases with numerous dependencies and intricate control flow can take some time to analyze and make this step slow.

Delays between writing code and running it are worth reducing. Aside from having small cost implications of dev time and CI/CD running expenses, there is a larger cost that is often overlooked: the human issue.

As humans, we love the creative process. Psychologically our desire to be creative, productive individuals means we bias *toward* the things we find most success in and err *away* from activity we experience friction from. Unfortunately this means that if a build process is slow, we subconsciously avoid doing it.

However, quality only occurs from feedback.

Static analysis helps raise quality by bringing large parts of the testing feedback cycle back within the creation process; but this feedback cycle is only of the code quality, not the quality of the UX flow or the suitability of the final product in market. Avoiding refining complex code can lead to it becoming even more complicated, or to it becoming less reliable. And so, far beyond being a simple convenience, it is in fact neurologically

© Ben Beattie-Hood 2023
B. Beattie-Hood, *Modern TypeScript*, https://doi.org/10.1007/978-1-4842-9723-0_7

imperative to keep your team's build-measure-learn time to a minimum, to help speed up feedback cycles – learning loops – and thereby improve the quality of your product, as well as your team's detailed understanding of it.

There are several steps in the build-measure-learn cycle – and they should all be kept as short and integrated as possible. Other books will deal with other aspects of this – how to reduce test execution time, how to improve data collection rate, how to improve ideation process – but in mastering TypeScript, we should ensure we understand how to improve its performance too.

This section is therefore dedicated to how to optimize the performance of your TypeScript configuration. We will cover how to utilize caching to store and reuse previously computed types; ways to increase caching and reduce computationally expensive inferred types and intersection types; and code partitioning strategies to permit incremental build. Lastly you will discover how to debug and isolate compilation performance issues in CPU and memory using some built-in and community tools for TypeScript.

To be able to optimize wisely (without overstepping per Knuth's principle) also ensures we understand the how of what we have built and is an important step to being a TypeScript expert.

Through the concepts covered in this chapter, you will gain a deep understanding of how to optimize TypeScript code for performance. By implementing these best practices, you can ensure that your TypeScript applications are more efficient to build and therefore more humanly likely to better maintain and scale in your product.

Reducing Inline Types

The first step in reducing any complex computation (such as, but not limited to, static type analysis) is to not do it. Caching allows us to store and reuse previously computed types and therefore is our first point of call in improving TypeScript performance.

Take the following code for example:

Listing 7-1. Simple identical anonymous types

```
const bob: {
    firstName: string
    lastName: string
} = getPerson('1');

const fred: {
    firstName: string
    lastName: string
} = getPerson('2');
```

In this code, you would've thought that TypeScript would be smart enough to recognize that the two pieces of code are the same and cache the anonymous type from the first piece of code to reuse for the second. But unfortunately it doesn't – it will instead go ahead and recalculate the type anew for both cases. This would be trivial in the preceding case, but when type computation starts to get complex involving intersections or inheritance, it starts to cost:

Listing 7-2. More complex identical anonymous types

```
function renderName(employee: { firstName: string, lastName:
string } &
    Dto<EmploymentRecord> & AnotherComplexType): string {
    return `${person.firstName} ${person.lastName}`;
}

function greet(person: { firstName: string, lastName:
string } &
    Dto<EmploymentRecord> & AnotherComplexType) {
    console.log('Hello ' + renderName(person));
}
```

```
greet({                        ⤶⚙
    firstName: 'Bob',
    lastName: 'Smith',
});
```

In the preceding code, TypeScript will compute the arg types for **greet** and check if the "bob smith" variable can be passed in – and then it will do it again inside the **greet** function when calling the **renderName** function!

So, as convenient as inline types are, the way to solve this is to always name your types. Assigning the complex type to a type alias or interface, TypeScript can cache and reuse the computation more easily, and in cases like the aforementioned, it will instead bypass the check entirely.

Listing 7-3. Store anonymous inline types as type aliases, and then reuse them to reduce recomputation

```
type Employee = { firstName: string, lastName: string } &
    Dto<EmploymentRecord> & AnotherComplexType;          ⤶⚙

function renderName(employee: Employee): string {   ⤶
                 Reuse type computation
    return `${person.firstName} ${person.lastName}`;
}

function greet(person: Employee) {                   ⤶
                 Reuse type computation
    console.log('Hello ' + renderName(person));      ⤶
                 Skip type assertion
}

greet({
    firstName: 'Bob',
    lastName: 'Smith',
});
```

Reducing Inferred Types

Another place TypeScript works extra hard is in inferred types. Take the following code for example:

Listing 7-4. A function with a complex inferred return type

```
function doSomethingComplex(x: any) {
    if (subcomputation1(x)) {
        return undefined;
    }
    if (subcomputation2(x)) {
        return true;
    }
    const a = 1000;
    if (subcomputation3(x)) {
        return a + Number(x);
    }
    throw new Error(x);
}

const foo = doSomethingComplex(bar); // what type is foo?
```

As a developer, if you were reading the code for **doSomethingComplex**, you can appreciate it would be hard to work out what the effective return type of a given value might be – and it's the same for TypeScript: it has to go through all the permutations in the function to work out the result. And doing it ourselves we can sympathize: it's fiddly, it takes time, and it uses up memory.

In contrast, if instead we explicitly set the function's return type, it would be easier to review the function and mentally check whether it conformed to the expected return value – and again it's the same for

TypeScript: reviewing the function with a pre-known return type is simpler and involves less dynamic interpretation of return type, skipping recomputation of return type as each return permutation is calculated.

Adding the return type also can help development: it's simpler for the consuming developer to read and understand without digging through the function's body or subfunctions, and it can also help provide a simple form of TDD to stub out the function's return type before adding the body, allowing TypeScript to help ensure all return cases are met.

The following example shows how setting the return type allows us to skip reading the function body as well as helps with a TDD approach ensuring we write the correct body that conforms to our conditional type:

Listing 7-5. Replacing inferred types with explicit types helps both the developer and the compiler

```
type SomethingComplexResult<X> =
    X extends undefined ? undefined
    : X extends (boolean | 'true' | 'false') ? true
    : X extends (NumericString | number) ? AsNumber<X>
    : never;

function doSomethingComplex<X>(x: X):
    SomethingComplexResult<X> {
// 🕵️ Stating a explicit return type means we don't need to
// understand all the body code to know what this function
// is up to 🕵️ 🕵️
    if (subcomputation1(x)) {
        return undefined;
    }
    if (subcomputation2(x)) {
        return true;
    }
```

```
    const a = 1000;
    if (subcomputation3(x)) {
        return a + Number(x);
    }
    if (subcomputation4(x)) {  // Plus the return type also helps
        return Date(x);  ✗     // detect when a return value
    }                          // doesn't match our expectations 🖐
    throw new Error(x);
}

const foo = doSomethingComplex("123" as const);
>    const foo = 123;    // And, TS can compute the type more
>                        // efficiently! 🎯
```

If you're still not sold on reducing inferred types (and, let's face it, they
are pretty handy for avoiding maintenance friction), there's one last reason
for ensuring return types on complex functions. And it has to do with
future support for concurrency.

Take the following example code:

Listing 7-6. A simple function with an inferred result that depends
on the result of further functions

```
function parse(s: string, mode: 'mode1' | 'mode2' | 'mode3') {
    switch (mode) {
        case 'mode1':
            return parser1(s);
        case 'mode2':
            return parser2(s); // calls parser1() or parser3()
                               // internally
```

```
        case 'mode3':
            return parser3(s); // calls parser1() or parser2()
                               // internally
    }
}
```

To infer the return type, TypeScript has to process each of the **parser()** functions. If these also have inferred return types and internally call each other, then the processing gets harder and harder to parallelize until essentially TypeScript has to resolve their return types sequentially (Figure 7-1).

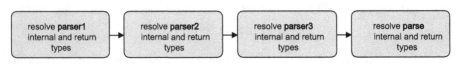

Figure 7-1. *Inferred return types mean parsing has to work sequentially*

Instead, adding the return type means each function can be analyzed in parallel, as the type contracts for the subfunctions are already available (Figure 7-2).

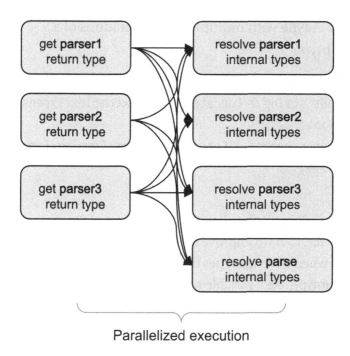

Parallelized execution

Figure 7-2. *Explicit return types mean parsing can be performed in parallel*

The official release of TypeScript doesn't currently leverage concurrency internally yet, but `https://github.com/microsoft/TypeScript/issues/30235` tracks progress and experiments on this, and alternative builds of TypeScript have also experimented with the idea, such as SWC's experimental STC compiler, or the OS Enzo project.

Inline Caching Using Conditional Types

Another helpful technique to aid caching of static analysis is to use the **infer** keyword to act like a temporary type variable (like a generic parameter). Take the following type:

Listing 7-7. A type with multiple recomputations of a complex subtype

```
type Foo<T> =
    T extends string ? Concatenate<Some<Complex<Expensive
    <Bar, T>>>, '-'>
    : T extends number ? Concatenate<Some<Complex<Expensive
    <Bar, T>>>, '.'>
    : T;
```

In the preceding type, we have computed part of the same expensive result type twice. Can we improve this? Happily, yes – we can use the inline type created when inferring types during pattern matching to store our computed subtype like a variable to use elsewhere in the type:

Listing 7-8. Caching a complex subtype in a conditional type inference

```
type Foo<T> =
    Some<Complex<Expensive<Bar, T>>>
    extends infer PrecomputedT  ⓥ Store complex type in a
    temporary type var
    ? (
        T extends string ? Concatenate<PrecomputedT, '-'>
        : T extends number ? Concatenate<PrecomputedT, '.'>
        : T
    )
    : never;
```

Reduce Intersections

Intersections are one of the more expensive computed types, because they merge properties creating resultant properties with the common-denominator subtype that satisfies both. In addition to this, TypeScript also performs further checks when resolving a value as the type because the value has to be checked against both properties, ending in slightly more than double the amount of computation (or triple or more in the case of multi-intersectional types).

Intersections are useful to reducing maintenance and when creating complex types, but they can also add cognitive overhead, where the property-merge is not really needed. Take the following example:

Listing 7-9. Simple intersections can have undesirable results where fields overlap

```
interface Employee {
    employeeNumber: number
    firstName: string
    lastName: string
    postcode: number
}

interface Person {
    name: string
    postcode: string
}

type EmployeeRecord = Person & Employee;

type Postcode = EmployeeRecord['postcode'];
>    type Postcode = never; 😔
```

223

In the preceding example, accidental overlap causes an error in the **postcode** field. To resolve this, you can use the **ShallowMerge** approach as shown in the following. But in the majority of cases, the overlap is better protected against rather than used as a feature.

Listing 7-10. ShallowMerge type that avoids overlapping fields

```
// Merge T and U together, but first omit all the overlapping
keys from T so
// that we don't have any merged fields. Effectively
the same as
// `const result = { ...t, ...u };`
// at runtime.

export type ShallowMerge<T, U> = Omit<T, keyof U> & U;
```

Interfaces, on the other hand, require resolution of all conflicting fields pre-compilation. The inheritance hierarchy of interfaces is also slightly simpler than intersection types, because of the requirement to resolve conflicts pre-compilation, and therefore, the relationships between interfaces can often be cached to improve build performance. And beyond anything else, much like an intersection type, interfaces can extend from multiple types, as follows:

Listing 7-11. Extending multiple types in an interface avoids the computation of merged fields that happens in intersections

```
interface EmployeeRecord extends Person, Omit<Employee,
'postcode'> {}

type Postcode = EmployeeRecord['postcode'];
>    type Postcode = string; 😄
```

Interfaces are therefore often safer and faster, and have less cognitive load, than intersection types. However, interfaces cannot extend types defined by their generic parameters, because they need to resolve all fields pre-compilation. So as a rule, use interfaces when combining known types, and use intersection types only when you need the property-merge effect and/or are combining types defined by generic parameters.

Reduce Union Types

Union types are incredibly important for avoiding invalid state, by attaching deeper values to otherwise simple enums. They come at a cost though, as values need to be checked against each value in the union to test that they are acceptable. This is fine with small enums, but when enums grow – especially via template literals – this checking can become exponentially heavy.

Therefore, reserve unions for where they are essential in your code, and consider using simple primitives (which are very fast to type-check) in cases where you are confident a union type has already effectively guarded.

Partition Using Packages and Projects
Partitioning Using Packages

Modern monorepo tooling, such as NX, allows common JavaScript patterns of multiple packages within the same repo to use caching between builds, reducing build (and even deploy) time greatly. This is the preferred approach to partitioning and is easiest to set up – just use the tool's built-in repo templating mechanism. See the "TypeScript Within a More Realistic Setup" section in Chapter 2.

Partitioning Using Projects

Prior to monorepos becoming more popular, TypeScript added a feature called **project references**, which are still available today. Similar to packages, but in TypeScript only, project references allow you to organize your code base into smaller, manageable projects and establish build dependencies between them. With project references, you can build and reference multiple TypeScript projects as a single unit, allowing build caching of those individual projects where changes have not occurred.

The following is a simple example configuration of TypeScript project references:

Listing 7-12. Using TypeScript project reference to reduce recompilation

```
// root/tsconfig.json:
{
    "compilerOptions": {
        "composite": true
    },
    "references": [
        { "path": './utils' },
        { "path": './app' },
    ]
}

// root/projects/utils/tsconfig.json:
{
    "compilerOptions": {
        "rootDir": "./src",
        "outDir": "../dist",
        "declaration": true
    },
```

```
    "include": [ "./src/**/*" ]
}

// root/projects/utils/src/index.ts
export function greet(name: string): string {
    return `Hello ${name}!`;
}

// root/projects/app/tsconfig.json:
{
    "compilerOptions": {
        "rootDir": "./src",
        "outDir": "../dist"
    },
    "references": [
        { "path": "../utils" }
    ],
    "include": [ "./src/**/*" ]
}

// root/projects/app/src/index.ts
import { greet } from 'utils';

const greeting = greet('James');
console.log(greeting);              // Outputs 'Hello James!'
```

When you build the **app** project, TypeScript will automatically build the utils project first due to the project reference. The resulting JavaScript files will be output to the specified **dist** folders. Changes in the **app** project only will not require the **utils** project to be rebuilt.

Other Performance Tweaks

TypeScript's **tsc** compiler includes a **--incremental** CLI parameter (or **"incremental": true** tsconfig option), which, when enabled, will cause it to store the compilation state in a **.tsbuildinfo** file. This file is used to determine the minimal set of files that may need to be re-evaluated or re-emitted since the last compilation, reducing the amount of build needed. You may also use the verbosely named **assumeChangesOnlyAffectDirectDependencies** suboption alongside this to even further reduce the recheck/rebuild effort of the compiler, at the expense of some exhaustivity.

Checking the .d.ts files within your node_modules packages is often pointless too, as – if you're using them – we'd assume they're bug-free. Therefore, TypeScript's **tsc** compiler includes **--skipDefaultLibCheck** and **--skipLibCheck** CLI parameters (**"skipDefaultLibCheck": true** and **"skipLibCheck": true** tsconfig options) to skip checking core libs (ECMAScript libs) and other node_modules packages, respectively.

Debugging Performance Issues

The preceding sections include a useful toolbelt of ways to ensure performance is good. But if it still isn't, then how do you find out the reason why?

Fortunately, TypeScript includes a suite of diagnostics that help us identify memory and CPU-intensive code. These diagnostics can be used to dump trace data during compilation, which can then be explored in a diagnostics viewer. To dump these diagnostics, use the CLI params as follows:

Listing 7-13. Command-line to save TypeScript extended diagnostics

```
npx tsc --extendedDiagnostics --generateTrace
./trace-dir --noEmit
```

Once the **tsc** process has completed, you will find it has created a folder called **./trace-dir** and stored two files inside it: **trace.json** and **types.json**.

Traces are complex data blobs and need tools to view them. So let's look at two tools we can use to do this.

Using the @typescript/analyze-trace NPM Package

We'll start with the easiest one. Run the following commands to install and run it:

Listing 7-14. Command-line to install and run TypeScript's analyze-trace tool

```
npm install --no-save @typescript/analyze-trace
npx analyze-trace ./trace-dir
```

The tool will output a list of "hot spots" in your code where compilation is taking more than average effort, as well as the time taken for each spot. This should be enough for you to get started targeting your performance optimizations.

Listing 7-15. Example output from TypeScript's analyze-trace tool

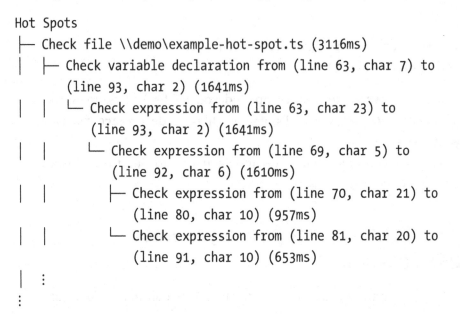

```
Hot Spots
├─ Check file \\demo\example-hot-spot.ts (3116ms)
│   ├─ Check variable declaration from (line 63, char 7) to
│       (line 93, char 2) (1641ms)
│   │   └─ Check expression from (line 63, char 23) to
│           (line 93, char 2) (1641ms)
│   │       └─ Check expression from (line 69, char 5) to
│               (line 92, char 6) (1610ms)
│   │           ├─ Check expression from (line 70, char 21) to
│                   (line 80, char 10) (957ms)
│   │           └─ Check expression from (line 81, char 20) to
│                   (line 91, char 10) (653ms)
│   ⋮
⋮
```

Using a Trace Viewer Within Your Browser

If you want to dig deeper, you can view the trace data in a trace viewer. Open a Chromium-based browser (such as Google Chrome or Edge), and enter **about:tracing** in the URL bar, and press enter. The browser will load a trace explorer view, where you can press the "Load" button shown in Figure 7-3 and choose the **trace.json** file, and the browser will display the trace data.

Figure 7-3. *Load your trace.json file by clicking this button*

When the trace has loaded, it will show a flame graph of the build process effort (y axis) against time (x axis). You can click on the root of each flame to see which file was processed at each point in a view panel at the bottom of the graph – choose the widest ones to find the highest processing cost.

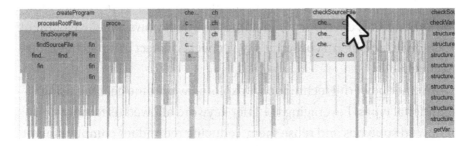

Figure 7-4. *The trace "flame graph" view*

Clicking on the flame graph row segments below each file root will show the effort given the code processed within that file (Figure 7-4). Unfortunately, the quick-view panel for this is less helpful: the types are only given ids (source type and target type), not names, so you'll need to locate the corresponding id in the **types.json** file to find the correlative type name, compilation mode (union, object, etc.), and recursion depth. It's a slower process than using the NPM package, but it allows more fine-grained analysis of what is happening during compilation.

Summary

In this chapter, we explored various techniques and best practices to optimize the performance of TypeScript compilation. Compilation performance is an important part of code build quality – if your code is a pain to build, as a human, you'll subconsciously avoid rebuilding it unless necessary, and this will reduce the velocity of your build-measure-learn cycle and the resultant quality of your code.

We covered how to reduce inline types' computational cost by utilizing caching. Caching allows us to store and reuse previously computed types, which can significantly improve performance, especially when dealing with complex type computations.

Next, we examined ways to reduce inferred types and the benefits of explicitly setting return types and other inferred types. By providing clear type annotations, developers can improve code reviews and development productivity and help TypeScript's type checker detect mismatches more effectively.

Another powerful technique we explored was inline caching using conditional types. Leveraging the infer keyword allowed us to store computed subtypes and reuse them, reducing redundant computations.

To optimize intersection types, we learned that interfaces often provide a safer, faster, and less cognitively burdensome alternative. However, we discussed specific cases where intersection types are beneficial, such as when merging properties is required.

Union types were also addressed, and we emphasized the importance of using them conscientiously to avoid excessive type-checking overhead where it could be avoided. Reserving union types for essential cases and using simpler primitives where code is already proven by outer types can improve performance significantly.

And we discussed partitioning strategies using packages and projects. Organizing code into smaller, manageable units not only improves build and compilation times but also enhances overall project maintainability.

Lastly, we reviewed how to debug compilation performance by using the extended diagnostics that can be output by the compiler. These diagnostics can be loaded into a community-contributed analytics package to output the hot spots in our compilation profile, or reviewed manually by using the trace viewer built into your browser.

By incorporating these performance optimizations into your TypeScript development workflow, you can ensure that their applications build efficiently, delivering a more rapidly iterable developer experience. This enablement of rapid iteration isn't a nice-to-have but actually impacts the code quality due to the way humans avoid painful (or boring) tasks such as extended wait times. And beyond even this, understanding when and how to apply these techniques contributes to a deeper comprehension of TypeScript as a language, enabling us to truly master the use of it in our projects.

CHAPTER 8

Build

Introduction

In this chapter, we will cover the remaining aspects of the build process. TypeScript project configuration is essential to this process, and the heart of this configuration lies in the **tsconfig.json** file, located in the root of your project folder. We'll begin with an overview of the main options available in this file. Understanding these options is crucial to successfully harness the full potential of the TypeScript compiler.

We will then cover what I would recommend you use as a sensible default for your **tsconfig.json** settings. Instead of overwhelming you with an exhaustive list of every option available, I'll highlight just the most important ones that will enhance your projects' code quality, maintainability, and compatibility.

After mastering the TypeScript compiler options, we explore additional tooling that can also help prevent errors available via linting. We will explore ESLint and its TypeScript ESLint supplement and again review what are a good go-to set of rules to leverage among the many available. By using the tsconfig and ESLint configurations in this chapter, you will have a robust tooling setup to catch the majority of common programming mistakes and improve code quality.

© Ben Beattie-Hood 2023
B. Beattie-Hood, *Modern TypeScript*, https://doi.org/10.1007/978-1-4842-9723-0_8

We will also look at another aspect of TypeScript compilation, which is support for the JSX format. You will see how JSX is just a syntactic sugar on top of normal JavaScript function calls and therefore how the type-safety techniques you have learned in this book can be applied to JSX code also.

Finally, we will explore an essential aspect of the build and deployment process: modules. Understanding the different module formats, and how TypeScript resolves modules, is crucial for making informed choices and managing code organization, dependencies, and interoperability when performing post-compilation steps like bundling and chunking. With this knowledge, you'll be able to structure your projects efficiently and take full advantage of TypeScript's module system.

By the end of this chapter, you will have gained a comprehensive understanding of TypeScript's build configurations, linting options, and the way it interacts with modules. This knowledge will be the final piece of the puzzle in becoming a true TypeScript expert.

Compiler Options

TypeScript project configuration is provided by the presence of a **tsconfig.json** file in the root of the project folder. To create a boilerplate of this file, use the following command:

Listing 8-1. Creating a default tsconfig.json file

```
npx tsc --init
```

The **tsconfig.json** file includes settings for the following:

> **Compiler options:** The tsconfig.json file allows you to specify various compiler options that control how TypeScript code is compiled. These options define the target ECMAScript version, module system, strictness level, output directory, and more.

Project structure: The tsconfig.json file helps define the structure of the TypeScript project. It specifies the root files or directories that should be included in the compilation process. It allows you to specify patterns for including or excluding files based on glob patterns.

Module resolution: TypeScript supports different module resolution strategies, such as Node.js, Classic, or Custom. The **tsconfig.json** file lets you configure the module resolution strategy for your project, which affects how TypeScript resolves and imports module dependencies. For details of module types, see the "Module Types Explained" section, later in this chapter.

Declaration files: Declaration files (**.d.ts**) provide type information for external JavaScript libraries or modules. The **tsconfig.json** file allows you to specify the generation of declaration files, their output directory, and other related settings.

Build configurations: In larger projects, you may have different build configurations for development, production, or other environments. The **tsconfig.json** file enables you to define multiple configurations by creating different tsconfig.json files and specifying the desired options for each configuration.

Recommended tsconfig.json Settings

Rather than going through all the settings available, which are easy to find on the TypeScript official website, we will now go through those compiler options I recommend you use.

In short, you should aim to use the following compiler options:

Listing 8-2. Recommended tsconfig.json settings for modern TypeScript projects

```
{
    "compilerOptions": {
        // Targeting Modern Browsers:
        "module": "ESNext",
        "moduleResolution": "NodeNext",
        "target": "ESNext",
        "lib": [ "esnext" ],

        // Prevent Optional Errors:
        "noEmitOnError": true,
        "strict": true,
        "strictNullChecks": true,
        "allowUnreachableCode": false,
        "noImplicitOverride": true,
        "noImplicitReturns": true,
        "noUncheckedIndexedAccess": true,
        "noUnusedLocals": true,
        "noUnusedParameters": true,
        "noFallthroughCasesInSwitch": true,
        "isolatedModules": true,
        "allowJs": true,
        "checkJs": true,
```

```
    // Display Complete Errors:
    "noErrorTruncation": true,

    // Enable Widest Range of Safe Interoperability:
    "downlevelIteration": true,
    "esModuleInterop": true,
    "allowSyntheticDefaultImports": true,
    "experimentalDecorators": true,
    "jsx": "react-jsx",

    // Project Structure and Build Output:
    "baseUrl": ".",
    "paths": {
        "src/*": [
            "src/*"
        ],
        "tests/*": [
            "tests/*"
        ],
    },
    "outDir": "dist",
  }
  "include": [
    "src/**/*.ts",
    "src/**/*.tsx",
    "src/**/*.d.ts",
    "tests/**/*.ts",
    "tests/**/*.tsx",
    "tests/**/*.d.ts",
  ],
```

```
    "exclude": [
        "node_modules"
    ]
}
```

The preceding configuration will target the newest browsers, save you from a range of optional errors, display complete errors, enable the widest range of safe interoperability, and lastly set your build project files structure to a standard configuration used by most projects. Phew – that's a lot! Let's go through these now to understand what they each do.

Targeting Modern Browsers

Why target only modern browsers? Don't we want a range of browsers or platforms to be able to load our code? Well, yes – we do. But the truth is that TypeScript isn't the best tool for this. It provides an acceptable output, but a much better output with easier definition can be achieved by using a post-build process such as **corejs** or **swc** against a **browserlist** aligned to your needs. See babel/preset-env (corejs) on `https://babeljs.io/`, presets on `https://swc.rs/`, and `https://browsersl.ist/` for more information on setting this build chain up, or use a bundler that includes downleveling such as parceljs (`https://parceljs.org/`). And for now, keep your TypeScript targeting only newer browsers, as follows:

> `module: "ESNext"`: Defines the module code generation for the emitted JavaScript. Using ESNext allows you to utilize ES modules, which offer better interoperability and support for tree shaking in modern JavaScript bundlers.

> `moduleResolution: "Node"`: Sets the strategy for resolving module dependencies. Choosing Node module resolution leverages the Node.js module resolution algorithm, which is widely adopted

and works well for most scenarios. The alternative "Classic" strategy only remains for backward compatibility and can be ignored for modern development. For more details on how TypeScript resolves modules using the Node setting, see the "How TypeScript Resolves Modules" section.

`target: "ESNext"`: Specifies the ECMAScript target version for the emitted JavaScript. By targeting ESNext, you can take advantage of the latest JavaScript features and syntax improvements, ensuring compatibility with modern environments.

`lib: ["esnext"]`: Specifies the library files to include during the compilation. In this case, only the esnext library is included, providing access to the features introduced in the ESNext ECMAScript version.

Prevent Optional Errors

noEmitOnError: true: With this setting, the compiler won't emit JavaScript files if there are any errors in the TypeScript code. It helps enforce stricter error checking and prevents generating potentially broken output files.

strict: true: Activating strict mode enables a set of strict type-checking options. Setting this to true actually enables a suite of different "sensible default" tests within TypeScript, including the following:

- `alwaysStrict`: Ensures that your files are parsed in the ECMAScript strict mode and emit "use strict" for each source file

- `noImplicitAny`: Prevents untyped cases where TypeScript would otherwise infer them as **any**. Ensures your devs explicitly set **any** when needed, which makes code review clearer

- `noImplicitThis`: Prevents untyped cases where TypeScript would otherwise need to infer **this** as **any**.

- `strictBindCallApply`: Prevents cases where TypeScript infers the built-in **call**, **bind**, and **apply** methods are called with untyped arguments

- `strictFunctionTypes`: Ensures tighter type checks on function arguments

- `strictNullChecks`: Ensures **null** and **undefined** have their own distinct types, and so a type error will be provided if you try to use optional or nullable values without asserting the value's existence first

- `strictPropertyInitialization`: Ensures all properties are correctly initialized during class construction, preventing accidental **undefined**s

- `useUnknownInCatchVariables`: Ensures you correctly interrogate or cast caught errors to known types before using them

Enabling this default check suite provided by the TypeScript compiler helps catch common programming mistakes, enhances code quality, and improves maintainability.

> `strictNullChecks: true`: When enabled, TypeScript enforces strict null checks, reducing the likelihood of null or undefined errors. It promotes safer programming practices by requiring explicit handling of nullable types.

> `allowUnreachableCode: false`: Set to false, TypeScript raises errors for any code after a non-avoidable return statement. This protects against mistakes in logic paths that may unwittingly prevent subsequent code from running.

`noImplicitOverride:` `true`: Set to true, ensures subclass overrides do not mistakenly override their superclass counterparts, instead requiring them to have an explicit override keyword. This makes it easier to see intent and check for errors during code review.

`noImplicitReturns:` `true`: Without this, ECMAScript permits functions to have logic branches that include no return value, instead inferring a final return value of **undefined** when the end of the function is reached. Enabled, this option prevents this and ensures all code paths provide a suitable return value.

`noUncheckedIndexedAccess:` `true`: When accessing indexed types, it adds **undefined** as a union case to any field not explicitly declared (and therefore made type-safe) against the type.

`noUnusedLocals:` `true`: This option flags any unused local variables as errors during compilation. It helps identify and remove redundant code, leading to cleaner and more efficient programs.

`noUnusedParameters:` `true`: Similar to **noUnusedLocals**, this option treats unused function parameters as errors. It encourages writing focused and concise functions by highlighting unused arguments.

`noFallthroughCasesInSwitch:` `true`: Generates an error when a switch statement has cases that fall through without appropriate break, return, or throw statements. It improves code clarity and reduces the chances of unintentional fallthrough.

isolatedModules: true: When enabled, each file is treated as a separate module, without sharing a global namespace. It encourages better encapsulation and helps prevent unintentional variable conflicts.

allowJs: true: This setting allows TypeScript to compile JavaScript files (.js) alongside TypeScript files (.ts). It provides flexibility for gradually adopting TypeScript in projects with existing JavaScript code.

checkJs: true: This setting, in conjunction with allowJs, ensures TypeScript processes any types inferable within JavaScript files.

Display Complete Errors

noErrorTruncation: true: When enabled, this option ensures that TypeScript displays the complete error messages without truncation. It helps in understanding and diagnosing errors more effectively.

Enable Widest Range of Safe Interoperability

downlevelIteration: true: This option enables the compiler to emit code compatible with downlevel iterations. It's useful when targeting older JavaScript environments that lack native support for iteration constructs like for...of loops.

`esModuleInterop: true`: When using CommonJS modules, this option simplifies interoperability with ES modules that use default imports or named imports. It allows for more seamless integration between different module systems.

`allowSyntheticDefaultImports: true`: When set to true, TypeScript allows importing modules that don't have default exports as if they had one. This simplifies the interoperation with legacy CommonJS modules and libraries that weren't designed with ES modules in mind.

`experimentalDecorators: true`: Enables support for the experimental decorators feature, which is used in conjunction with libraries like Angular or TypeScript transformers. This option allows using decorators for class and property declarations.

`jsx: "react-jsx"`: Enables support for JSX syntax (see the "JSX/TSX" section) using the modern, runtime-agnostic output format. Initially, JSX output in TypeScript was tied to React (or React-likes, such as Preact), but this newer approach outputs to a simple **__jsx()** function call, which can be defined by a wider range of runtime frameworks.

Project Structure and Build Output

baseUrl and **paths**: These options allow you to configure module resolution for custom module paths. "baseUrl" specifies the base directory used for resolving nonrelative module names, while "paths" define mappings from module names to specific directories or files.

outDir: If you are not using a bundler and want TypeScript to output (a.k.a. "emit") JavaScript files, you'll need them saved somewhere. By default, the compiled files are emitted as siblings to each of their originating TypeScript files, which is actually pretty useless; **outDir** allows you to specify a more useful, specific, location for the resultant output. However, if you *are* using a bundler, you may instead want to switch on **noEmit:true**, to use TypeScript for type checking only and rely on a different transpiler such as swc or babel (with corejs) to emit the output file(s).

include and **exclude**: **include** allows you to provide an array of globs of the entrypoint files you want to include in the compilation. Any files referenced *from* these files will also be included, so we can also **exclude** a "node_modules" glob to ignore traversing deeper into any packages we aren't creating ourselves.

Other Options

The only remaining options I would suggest considering would be the performance-related options **skipLibCheck**, **skipDefaultLibCheck**, and **incremental**, as well the diagnostic **diagnostics/extendedDiagnostics** options. These are all covered in Chapter 7, in the "Other Performance Tweaks" and "Debugging Performance Issues" sections.

Linting

Linting is most often used as a way to enforce code style decisions across a team, or even just in your own code. But this isn't the true extent of what lint tools such as ESLint can bring to your development process.

Linting, simply put, is actually a static-analysis step that runs a suite of rules on your code. In this light, the TypeScript type checks themselves can be considered a lint ruleset. And using community-contributed tools such as ESLint, we can extend those type checks to include additional safety checks that haven't officially been made part of TypeScript yet.

ESLint comes with a suite of rules that it recommends as best practice. On top of these, the TypeScript team and the community have contributed a further suite of rules in the supplementary NPM package. We will review these in this chapter and list those ones that will assist with further type assertions.

Installing ESLint

First, to install ESLint and its TypeScript ESLint supplement, run the following command in the root of your project:

Listing 8-3. Installing ESLint and associated TypeScript plug-ins

```
npm install --save-dev
  @typescript-eslint/parser
  @typescript-eslint/eslint-plugin
  eslint
  typescript
```

The rules available in these tools are provided through ESLint plug-ins. To configure these, we now need to create a **.eslintrc.cjs** file in the root of our project and with the following code:

Listing 8-4. A normal ESLint configuration for TypeScript

```
// /.eslintrc.cjs:

/* eslint-env node */
module.exports = {
    extends: [
        'eslint:recommended',
        'plugin:@typescript-eslint/recommended'
    ],
    parser: '@typescript-eslint/parser',
    plugins: [
        '@typescript-eslint'
    ],
    root: true,
};
```

The preceding configuration will tell ESLint to use its own default "recommended" suite of rules, as well as the "recommended" ones provided in the **typescript-eslint** plug-in.

Ideal Ruleset

In many situations, devs will consider the aforementioned a sufficient coverage. But some of the rules included in the recommended sets are either better delivered by TypeScript itself or can be considered stylistic. Others are not included in the recommended sets yet because of the additional processing power they require, but are worth bringing into your project if possible. So let's edit your **.eslintrc.cjs** now to the following more powerful setup:

Listing 8-5. Recommended ESLint configuration for TypeScript

```
/* eslint-env node */
module.exports = {
    extends: [
        'eslint:recommended',
        'plugin:@typescript-eslint/recommended',
        'plugin:@typescript-eslint/recommended-requiring-type-
        checking'
    ],
    parser: '@typescript-eslint/parser',
    parserOptions: {
        project: './tsconfig.json',
        ecmaVersion: 2022,
        sourceType: 'module',
        createDefaultProgram: true,
        ecmaFeatures: {
            tsx: true,
        },
    },
    plugins: [
        '@typescript-eslint'
    ],
    root: true,
    rules: {
        '@typescript-eslint/default-param-last': 'error',
        '@typescript-eslint/no-array-constructor': 'off',
        '@typescript-eslint/no-empty-function': 'off',
        '@typescript-eslint/no-empty-interface': 'off',
        '@typescript-eslint/no-explicit-any': 'off',
        '@typescript-eslint/no-extra-non-null-
        assertion': 'off',
```

```
'@typescript-eslint/no-extra-semi': 'off',
'@typescript-eslint/no-implied-eval': 'error',
'@typescript-eslint/no-inferrable-types': 'off',
'@typescript-eslint/no-invalid-this': 'error',
'@typescript-eslint/no-loop-func': 'warn',
'@typescript-eslint/no-loss-of-precision': 'warn',
'@typescript-eslint/no-misused-new': 'off',
'@typescript-eslint/no-non-null-assertion': 'off',
'@typescript-eslint/no-redeclare': 'error',
'@typescript-eslint/no-shadow': [
    'warn',
    { allow: ['_'] },
],
'@typescript-eslint/no-unnecessary-type-
assertion': 'warn',
'@typescript-eslint/no-unsafe-argument': 'off',
'@typescript-eslint/no-unsafe-assignment': 'off',
'@typescript-eslint/no-unsafe-call': 'off',
'@typescript-eslint/no-unsafe-member-access': 'off',
'@typescript-eslint/no-unsafe-return': 'off',
'@typescript-eslint/no-unused-vars': 'off',
'@typescript-eslint/prefer-namespace-keyword': 'off',
'@typescript-eslint/prefer-nullish-coalescing': 'warn',
'@typescript-eslint/require-array-sort-compare': [
    'error',
    { ignoreStringArrays: true },
],
'@typescript-eslint/require-await': 'warn',
'@typescript-eslint/restrict-template-expressions': [
    'error',
    {
```

```
        allowAny: false,
        allowBoolean: true,
        allowNullish: false,
        allowNumber: true,
        allowRegExp: false,
    },
],
'constructor-super': 'off',
'for-direction': 'off',
'getter-return': 'off',
'guard-for-in': 'warn',
'no-async-promise-executor': 'off',
'no-await-in-loop': 'warn',
'no-caller': 'error',
'no-class-assign': 'off',
'no-compare-neg-zero': 'off',
'no-console': [
    'warn',
    { allow: ['warn', 'error'] },
],
'no-const-assign': 'off',
'no-control-regex': 'off',
'no-delete-var': 'off',
'no-dupe-args': 'off',
'no-dupe-class-members': 'off',
'no-dupe-keys': 'off',
'no-eval': 'warn',
'no-floating-decimal': 'warn',
'no-func-assign': 'off',
'no-implicit-globals': 'warn',
'no-import-assign': 'off',
```

```
'no-iterator': 'error',
'no-labels': 'error',
'no-multi-str': 'warn',
'no-new-func': 'error',
'no-new-symbol': 'off',
'no-obj-calls': 'off',
'no-octal-escape': 'error',
'no-octal': 'error',
'no-param-reassign': 'error',
'no-proto': 'error',
'no-redeclare': 'off',
'no-return-assign': [
    'warn',
    'always',
],
'no-self-compare': 'error',
'no-sequences': 'error',
'no-setter-return': 'off',
'no-sparse-arrays': 'off',
'no-template-curly-in-string': 'error',
'no-this-before-super': 'off',
'no-throw-literal': 'warn',
'no-undef': 'off',
'no-unreachable': 'off',
'no-unused-vars': 'off',
'no-useless-call': 'warn',
'no-useless-rename': 'warn',
'no-var': 'error',
'no-warning-comments': 'warn',
'no-with': 'off',
'prefer-promise-reject-errors': 'warn',
```

```
        'symbol-description': 'error',
        'valid-typeof': 'off',
        'vars-on-top': 'warn',
    }
};
```

Phew! That's a lot of settings. Let's review these changes now and discuss each.

Additional Strict Errors

@typescript-eslint/ default-param-last	Default parameters are parameters that are assigned a specific default value when unspecified by a caller. Without enforcing defaults to be at the end, parameter assignment can be confusing.
@typescript-eslint/ no-implied-eval	Some JavaScript methods, such as setTimeout, allow a string rather than a function to be passed as their callback parameter. This can be a security concern, and therefore, we want to prevent it.
@typescript-eslint/ no-invalid-this	JavaScript follows a functional paradigm, and therefore, functions can be "bound" to a value and called. However, in most cases, this is just confusing, as the **this** parameter is usually simpler to pass as a simple arg – directly or via a currying library if necessary. This rule enforces that functions do not use the **this** keyword if not part of a class.
@typescript-eslint/ no-redeclare	Ensures a stricter extension approach extending interfaces, ensuring that redeclared fields are of the same type and therefore not mistakenly overridden.

(continued)

@typescript-eslint/ require-array-sort- compare	In JavaScript, array's **.sort** method actually does a string comparison of each of the items – which is fine if your array is of strings, but otherwise will internally convert them to strings by calling **.toString()** on each value before comparison. The results are therefore usually undesired (e.g., number arrays become sorted lexicographically rather than by magnitude). To avoid this, this rule ensures we specify a comparison function when sorting.
@typescript-eslint/ restrict-template- expressions	JavaScript template literals can contain any value in their expressions, and on each a **.toString()** function is called before incorporating into the template output. This is fine for many primitives, but values such as objects, or undefined, or symbols are instead included in an unhelpful way (e.g., "Hello [object Object]!"). This rule ensures we convert values beforehand, thereby avoiding errors.
no-caller	ECMAScript's **arguments.caller** and **arguments. callee** make some code optimizations impossible and also complicate your code. This rule disallows the use of these values.
no-iterator	Disallows the use of a legacy **__iterator__** property – if you wanted this, you should probably use the new ECMAScript iterables, for a simpler control flow.
no-labels	Labels and their correlative **break** (goto) statements make control flow difficult to reason about, introducing an additional layer of statefulness that makes testing hard. This rule disallows the use of labels.

(continued)

no-new-func	To simplify code readability, the **new** keyword should be restricted to use for constructing classes. This rule ensures this keyword isn't used against functions, which can make it difficult to debug and reason about the types returned by and used internally within those functions.
no-octal-escape **&** **no-octal**	Earlier versions of JavaScript required octal escape sequences for extended character sets. Many developers are not familiar with these and are more comfortable now with the more modern Unicode escape sequences. This rule ensures no octal escape sequences are used.
no-param-reassign	The use of parameters as reassignable variables inside functions can lead to confusing behavior, such as mutation of the inbuilt **arguments** object and/or counterintuitive execution flow. This rule ensures no parameters are reassigned and is somewhat correlative to **no-var**, described later in this section.
no-proto	The use of the inbuilt **__proto__** property has been deprecated since ECMAScript 3.1. This rule ensures this property is not used in your code.
no-self-compare	Comparing a value to itself (e.g., **if (person === person))** is both pointless as well as usually a mistake. This rule ensures this is prohibited in your code.

(continued)

no-sequences	Comma operators in JavaScript allow multiple expressions to occur in a single line in some special situations. However, they are more confusing to reason about than simple control flows and therefore can lead to errors. This rule prevents the comma operator being used and thereby avoids these potential control-flow errors.
no-template-curly-in-string	String templates use **${}** syntax to load in their template values. The use of this syntax in a nontemplate string (i.e., a string delimited by " or ' characters) is usually a typo, and therefore, this rule protects you from these typos.
no-var	The original ECMAScript **var** keyword only respects function scope and ignores scopes more often used in other languages such the scopes provided by the **while**, **if**, or **for** keyword. As a solution, **const** and **let** were brought into ECMAScript v6 onward, and so this rule disallows the **var** keyword in preference to these newer, safer approaches.
symbol-description	Anonymous symbols are hard to debug and locate in code. This rule ensures all your symbols are given descriptions when constructing them.

Additional Strict Warnings

`@typescript-eslint/` `no-loop-func`	This rule protects against bad closures within functions. Functions mistakenly enclosing vars (rather than scoped lets or consts) can have these values updated outside their scope, and so protecting against these helps avoid unanticipated errors.

`@typescript-eslint/`
`  no-loss-of-`
`precision`
	Numbers in JavaScript have a finite number of digits – which means that as you start to use large floats or high-precision floats beyond a certain number of columns, JavaScript will start to automatically round them! This lint check protects you against this by ensuring high-precision values are stored in types that can handle it.

`@typescript-eslint/` `no-shadow`	Declaring a variable within a function that has the same name as a variable in the scope surrounding the function is called variable "shadowing." It doesn't cause errors, but reasoning in the code can become very difficult, especially when both internal and external values are needed. This rule ensures you name your variables uniquely across scopes, preventing shadowing.

`@typescript-eslint/`
`  no-unnecessary-`
`type-assertion`
	This rule is included in the typescript-eslint recommended set but is set to "error", which is too severe. Setting it to warn allows you to use type assertions as you prefer but flags them as optionally removable if they are extraneous.

(continued)

@typescript-eslint/ prefer-nullish- coalescing	In JavaScript, you can coalesce falsy values using the || operator. As undefined and null are both counted falsy, it can be tempting to use the || operator to coalesce these too; but modern ECMAScript provides a dedicated operator **??** for this instead, making the code's intent clearer.
@typescript-eslint/ require-await	There's no point marking a function with the **async** keyword if it doesn't include at least one **await** statement – it's either an error or a false function signature. This rule ensures this is detected and flagged.
guard-for-in	In JavaScript, it's possible to write a **for** statement with no exit clause. This is nearly always a mistake, as it provides an infinite loop. This rule protects against this in your code.
no-await-in-loop	While you can call **await** inside a loop, it's usually better to instead use **Promise.all** to execute the operations in parallel. The main scenario where you'd want to use an await in a loop is in an async generator function that is looping over another async generator – and as this is so infrequent, then we protect against accidents by enabling this rule.
no-console	The **console.log** variants (log, debug, warn, error) are useful for investigating bugs and checking control flow. However, it's important to remove these before you ship your code to production, so this rule allows us to check for these calls. We have set our rule to allow warn and error logs though, which are rarely used explicitly when debugging, as these are more likely to be legitimate outputs in your code for logging nonfatal runtime conditions.

(*continued*)

no-eval	The **eval** statement in JavaScript is widely considered a security risk, as it can allow accidental behavior injection that is hard to sanitize against. This rule prevents the use of **eval** to protect against these security errors.
no-floating-decimal	ECMAScript permits floating decimals to be defined in code without a leading or trailing zero (e.g., **.8** instead of **0.8**, or **1** instead of **1.0**). However, without a leading or trailing zero, these decimal operators are hard to spot and can also be typos; and so this rule prevents these by flagging them as errors.
no-implicit-globals	Global variables are intrinsically hard to reason about, as every operation across your program can read and write to them. As such, they add statefulness to every function and so massively increase the complexity and undermine the exhaustive testability of your program. However, they are sometimes a necessary evil; but being such should need to be declared explicitly rather than implicitly and therefore potentially by accident. This rule ensures explicit statement of global vars and protects against this concern.
no-multi-str	The backslash character can escape special chars in strings. You can backslash apostrophes, quotes, tabs, and others to ensure they are included literally rather than interpreted as the string. One of the chars you can backslash (an undocumented feature) is the newline char itself (actual newline, rather than \n). This is usually seen as bad practice as it can confuse readability, and the \n approach is more canonical. This rule prevents the intentional or accidental use of escaped newlines.

(continued)

no-return-assign	Assignments in JavaScript all actually return a value, and one of the quirks of this means that you can write **return x=y+1** validly in a function. However, this is rarely needed unless x is global, and in practice, usually it represents a typo of **return x===y+1**. This rule prevents this form of typos.
no-throw-literal	In JavaScript, any given value can be thrown – errors, strings, numbers, nulls, booleans – anything! Unpacking these values in a catch statement can therefore be very difficult. Narrowing the variance by enforcing that only errors (and subclasses of errors) can be thrown at least means that errors include a readable toString and some other expected error data.
no-useless-call	This is an edge case, but this prevents unnecessary calls to the inbuilt functional **.call** and **.apply** methods where a direct call would have the same effect. Admittedly in practice, you're unlikely to trigger this rule, but it'll keep unnecessary curly code at bay.
no-useless-rename	When refactoring in an IDE, renaming a variable (F2 in VSCode) will, due to a limitation in the tooling, lead to unnecessary import statements such as **import { x as x } from 'x.js'**. This rule will protect against these.
no-warning-comments	Conventional tags such as **fixme** and **todo** in comments will be flagged by this so that these human-recognized issues are logged with your other static analysis.

(*continued*)

prefer-promise-reject-errors	Similar to **no-throw-literal**, this rule ensures that only Error classes are passed into **Promise.reject()** calls, making try/catch handling simpler and more reliable.
vars-on-top	This is a backup to the **no-var** rule, ensuring that if you really do need to use vars, they are at least only in the outermost scope, which makes them slightly easier to reason about.

Removed Rules

In addition to switching on some additional rules in the preceding config, we also switched some of the "recommended" rules *off*. There are two groups of reasons for these. For those in the typescript-eslint plug-in, newer versions of TypeScript already provide safer checking than the ruleset does, and so we no longer need them. And for those in the ESLint config (further down in the following table), they are simply already covered by existing TypeScript error checks and type safety, so they are also no longer needed.

@typescript-eslint/ **no-array-constructor**	Older versions of TypeScript may not have checked for this, but all newer versions do automatically, so this rule is no longer needed.
@typescript-eslint/ **no-empty-function**	TypeScript return types and type inference essentially mitigate this, and sometimes, no-op functions are needed, so this rule is not useful.
@typescript-eslint/ **no-empty-interface**	TypeScript's own type inference mitigates this rule.

(continued)

261

@typescript-eslint/ no-explicit-any	As discussed previously, there are cases in advanced usage where you will need to use the **any** type in your code. Having this type in your code is already visible during peer review, and so there is no need to also have additional inline rule setting stating "eslint-disable no-explicit-any".
@typescript-eslint/ no-extra-non-null- assertion	In newer versions of TypeScript, extra non-null assertions are optimized out during the TypeScript compilation process, so this is unneeded.
@typescript-eslint/ no-extra-semi	This rule is not actually impactful on the operation of your code and can be considered stylistic. By all means, keep it if you'd like the linting process to clean up any spare semicolons, but you may not need this cleaning if you are already using an alternative formatter like Prettier or Rome.
@typescript-eslint/ no-inferrable-types	As with **@typescript-eslint/no-unnecessary-type-assertion** in the warn rules, it is sometimes desirable to explicitly state a type that can also be inferred – either during refactoring, to improve compilation performance, or just as preference.
@typescript-eslint/ no-misused-new	TypeScript itself prevents the same misuse around the **new** keyword that this rule aims to prevent, so this is unneeded.
@typescript-eslint/ no-non-null- assertion	TypeScript type inference automatically prevents misuse of the non-null assertion in a more graceful way, so we can disable this rule.
@typescript-eslint/ no-unsafe-argument	TypeScript will cover this in the majority of cases; and the ESLint rule has had bugs around some optional args cases, so we can disable this for now.

(continued)

@typescript-eslint/ no-unsafe- assignment	As with **@typescript-eslint/no-explicit- any** sometimes in advanced usage, it is beneficial to assert a known value as **any** in order to perform further operations on it. Explicitly asserting it as **any** is sufficient for any PR conversations to be had.
@typescript-eslint/ no-unsafe-call	TypeScript itself already covers unsafe callsites, and this rule also appears to have a bug in some inferred cases, so we can safely disable it.
@typescript-eslint/ no-unsafe-member- access	As with the aforementioned, TypeScript itself already covers unsafe member access too, and (similarly) this rule also appears to have a bug in some inferred cases, so we can safely disable it too.
@typescript-eslint/ no-unsafe-return	TypeScript type inference already provides sufficient guardrails around return values by inferring and propagating their types into their assigned values, so we can safely disable this rule also.
@typescript-eslint/ no-unused-vars	TypeScript provides this more accurately, so long as you switch on the tsconfig.json noUnusedLocals setting (see the "Compiler Options" section, covered previously in this chapter), so this rule is unneeded. However, we do use the ESLint **no-var** rule – see the "Additional Strict Errors" section.
@typescript-eslint/ prefer-namespace- keyword	This is a stylistic rule, and as it encourages support of the legacy **namespace** approach to module scoping (now largely deprecated), we can switch this off as extraneous.
constructor-super	TypeScript natively catches this already with error codes ts(2335) and ts(2377), and so this JavaScript- specific ESLint rule is not needed.

(continued)

263

for-direction	This rule is useful but is actually stylistic, so we'll switch it off.
getter-return	TypeScript covers this already with error code ts(2378), and so this JavaScript-specific ESLint rule is not needed.
no-async-promise-executor	TypeScript type checking ensures correct unwrapping of nested promises, and so this JavaScript rule isn't a concern for us.
no-class-assign	JavaScript allows assigning a class name to a variable value – TypeScript saves the day again, preventing this sort of silliness by using type enforcement and error code ts(2629).
no-compare-neg-zero	TypeScript covers this already with error code ts(2367), and so this JavaScript-specific ESLint rule is not needed.
no-const-assign	TypeScript covers this already with error code ts(2588), and so this JavaScript-specific ESLint rule is not needed.
no-control-regex	This rule is stylistic, and you may want to consider the use of it, but it is not included in our focus on error removal.
no-delete-var	TypeScript covers this already with error code ts(2703), and so this JavaScript-specific ESLint rule is not needed.
no-dupe-args	TypeScript covers this already with error code ts(2300), and so this JavaScript-specific ESLint rule is not needed.

(continued)

no-dupe-class-members	TypeScript covers this already with error codes ts(2393) and ts(2300), and so this JavaScript-specific ESLint rule is not needed.
no-dupe-keys	TypeScript covers this already with error code ts(1117), and so this JavaScript-specific ESLint rule is not needed.
no-func-assign	TypeScript covers this already with error code ts(2539), and so this JavaScript-specific ESLint rule is not needed.
no-import-assign	TypeScript covers this already with error codes ts(2539) and ts(2540), and so this JavaScript-specific ESLint rule is not needed.
no-new-symbol	TypeScript covers this already with error code ts(2350), and so this JavaScript-specific ESLint rule is not needed.
no-obj-calls	TypeScript covers this already with error code ts(2349), and so this JavaScript-specific ESLint rule is not needed.
no-redeclare	TypeScript covers this already with error code ts(2451), and so this JavaScript-specific ESLint rule is not needed.
no-setter-return	TypeScript covers this already with error code ts(2408), and so this JavaScript-specific ESLint rule is not needed.
no-sparse-arrays	TypeScript removes the impact of these during compilation, and so there's no performance risk of using sparse arrays, so we don't need this rule.

(continued)

no-this-before-super	TypeScript covers this already with error code ts(2376), and so this JavaScript-specific ESLint rule is not needed.
no-undef	TypeScript covers this already with error code ts(2304), and so this JavaScript-specific ESLint rule is not needed.
no-unreachable	TypeScript covers this already with error code ts(7027), and so this JavaScript-specific ESLint rule is not needed – although you must set the **allowUnreachableCode: false** flag in your tsconfig.json to ensure this.
no-unused-vars	TypeScript can cover this if you set the **allowUnusedLocals** and **allowUnusedParameters** to false in your tsconfig.json, and will otherwise remove these during compilation anyway, so they have no actual impact and this rule is therefore not needed.
no-with	TSC provides this by default.
valid-typeof	TypeScript covers this already with error code ts(2367), and so this JavaScript-specific ESLint rule is not needed.
getter-return	TypeScript covers this already with error code ts(2378), and so this JavaScript-specific ESLint rule is not needed.

Further Rules

ESLint is a powerful tool to add to your build workflow, adding many checks that are not yet part of the TypeScript type-checking analysis. It represents an important aspect of your build process and should be part of every TypeScript project to augment and protect against errors.

As you may have noticed, in all the cases we've discussed in this section, we are focusing our lint checking on rules that prevent *actual errors* in our code. This type of static analysis is important to reduce the maintenance effort on your team. And if you wish to go further, additional suites of these error-prevention rules are also available in the following rulesets that ship with the **typescript-eslint** package:

- **plugin:@typescript-eslint/strict**

- **plugin:@typescript-eslint/strict-type-checked**

Beyond these error-prevention rules, you may also wish to review *stylistic* rules across your organization or within your teams. However, in most cases, I'd recommend treading lightly with these stylistic rules, and instead let teams largely determine their own, as these stylistic settings relate more to opinion than runtime impact.

The **typescript-eslint** package also includes some further stylistic rulesets too (**stylistic** and **stylistic-type-checked**), which may also be helpful as they align to most coding practices in larger orgs, and you can (as we have for error checks) always customize further to define your own "sensible defaults."

JSX/TSX

JSX, which stands for JavaScript XML, is an extension to the JavaScript language. It allows the developer to write HTML-like syntax directly within JavaScript code, combining the power of JavaScript and the flexibility of

HTML together, and is written in files with a **.jsx** file extension. TSX is an extension of JSX, bringing TypeScript type checking to JSX, and so it is written in files with a (you guessed it!) **.tsx** extension.

Here's an example of the JSX/TSX syntax:

Listing 8-6. Example of JSX and TSX syntax

```
const element = <h1>Hello, world!</h1>;
```

Most browsers and runtimes won't be able to run this directly, and so during build, this is actually transpiled to the following:

Listing 8-7. Resulting code emitted from Listing 8-6

```
const element = _jsx("h1", { children: "Hello, world!" });
```

Whatever JSX runtime you have configured (the default is React) will have provided a function called **_jsx** to the global scope, and so the preceding code will call this function. This JSX runtime function will then essentially correlate your input arguments with an internal structure called a Virtual DOM and then use this to synchronize your changes to the actual browser DOM so that your **<h1>Hello, world!</h1>** is displayed as a real HTML H1 with text content in your browser.

For the curious, the reason your changes aren't written directly to the browser DOM is that changes to the browser DOM are relatively expensive in terms of processor and memory, as they involve layout, repainting, removing/attaching event handlers, and many other things. The Virtual DOM, on the other hand, can be cheaply mutated, and then only the changes are synchronized across.

Let's now see an example of adding our own component to the syntax. We do this by creating a function and naming it using Pascal case (i.e., its name needs to start with an uppercase first letter):

Listing 8-8. Creating and using a React component in TSX syntax

```
interface MyComponentProps {}

const MyComponent: React.FC<PropsWithChildren<MyComponentPro
ps>> = (props) => {
    return (
        <div>
            {props.children}
        </div>
    )
}

const element = <MyComponent>Hello, world!</MyComponent>
```

Now, take a look at what that compiles into:

Listing 8-9. Resulting code emitted from Listing 8-8

```
const MyComponent = (props) => {
    return (_jsx("div", { children: props.children }));
};
const element = _jsx(MyComponent, { children: "Hello, world!" });
```

Normal ECMAScript convention is to name functions and variables with a lowercase first letter (called camelCase, because it has a hump in the middle). Naming the function in Pascal case triggers the compiler to record the function as a JSX receiver. When the transpiler then spots the receiver in the JSX element name, it will use your function as an argument for the **_jsx** runtime function. Internally, the **_jsx** runtime function will then effectively do this:

Listing 8-10. How the TSX _jsx runtime function works internally

```
function _jsx(component, props) {
    // ...
    const renderedComponent = component(props);
    // ...
}
```

You may also notice in the preceding example that the props being passed in are an object, and any JSX children components are passed in via a property automatically named **children** by the transpiler.

Because we now know that all JSX components are simple function calls, then of course we can also define our own properties alongside the automatic **children** property:

Listing 8-11. Passing parameters to our component, which come through as function arguments

```
interface MyComponentProps {
    imageSrc: string
}

const MyComponent: React.FC<PropsWithChildren<MyComponentPro
ps>> = (props) => {
    return (
        <div>
            <img src={props.imageSrc} />
            {props.children}
        </div>
    )
}
```

```
const element =
    <MyComponent imageSrc="assets/greeting.png">
        Hello, world!
    </MyComponent>
```

And we can even redefine the type of the **children** property and require only a specific type of children:

Listing 8-12. Defining types requiring specific children in our React component

```
interface AnimalComponentProps {
    name: string
    type: 'amphibian' | 'bird' | 'fish' | 'mammal' | 'reptile'
}
const AnimalComponent: React.FC<AnimalComponentProps> =
(props) => {
    return (
        <div>
            {props.firstName} {props.lastName}
        </div>
    )
}

interface MyComponentProps {
    imageSrc: string
    children: ReactElement<AnimalComponentProps>[]
}

const MyComponent: React.FC<React.PropsWithChildren<MyComponent
Props>> = (props) => {
    return (
        <div>
            <img src={props.imageSrc} />
```

```
            {props.children}
        </div>
    )
}

const element =
    <MyComponent imageSrc="assets/animals.png">
        <AnimalComponent name="Garfield" type="mammal" />
        <AnimalComponent name="Nemo" type="fish" />
        <AnimalComponent name="Tweetie" type="bird" />
    </MyComponent>;
```

Or to require a function as a child:

Listing 8-13. Defining our children as a more powerful function rather than a simple JSX node

```
interface MyComponentProps {
    imageSrc: string
    children:
      (args: { greetingName: string }) => ReactElement<Animal
      ComponentProps>[]
}

const MyComponent: React.FC<React.PropsWithChildren<MyComponent
Props>> = (props) => {
    return (
        <div>
            <img src={props.imageSrc} />
            {props.children({ greetingName: 'World' })}
        </div>
    )
}
```

```
const element =
    <MyComponent imageSrc="assets/animals.png">
        {(({ greetingName }) =>

            Hello, {greetingName}!
            <AnimalComponent name="Garfield"
            type="mammal" />
            <AnimalComponent name="Nemo" type="fish" />
            <AnimalComponent name="Tweetie" type="bird" />

        }
    </MyComponent>;
```

Lastly, as components in JSX/TSX are simple function calls, we can also provide generic parameters to them (or have them infer generic parameters), much the same as normal function calls:

Listing 8-14. Using generics in TSX

```
interface MyListProps<Item> {
    items: Item[]
    onPress: (item: Item) => void
}

const MyList = <Item,>(props: MyListProps<Item>) => {
    // ...
}

const items = useMemo(() => [1, 2, 3], []);
const onPressHandler = useCallback((item: number) => { /* ...
*/ }, []);
const element =
```

```
<MyList<number>
    items={items}
    onPress={onPressHandler}
/>;
```

Note   Notice that I've used a "," after the generic parameter. This is a handy trick to help TypeScript know that the generic parameter list is not to be confused with a JSX/TSX element.

Modules

Module Types Explained

Prior to ECMAScript Modules (ESM), modules were just conventions around closures in JavaScript files. As outlined in this book's introduction, these evolved from emerging needs over the course of time, and TypeScript has added output support for each of these as they were released. However, as the industry has grown, and additional techniques such as bundling, chunking, and zero-js delivery have emerged, the TypeScript team's development has necessarily focused more on type checking, the core team instead contributing to Babel's TypeScript "preset", in order to not lag on the pace of change. However, it is still worth having a basic appreciation of these underlying module types, as these are still part of the module resolution process and therefore part of TypeScript compilation and present in the **tsconfig.json** options.

To demonstrate, take the following example snippet of TypeScript code. In each following section, we will review the same code transpiled by TypeScript to each module system, so you can see how the closure conventions work in each case:

Listing 8-15. Example of a simple module written in TypeScript

```
import { URL } from 'node:url';
export function createUrl(href: string) {
    return new URL(href);
}
```

CommonJS (CJS)

Created in 2009 to solve the lack of a native ECMAScript module system at that time and adopted by the Node.js core team while still in its infancy. This format is still supported by many bundlers (e.g., Webpack, Rollup), but gradually the industry is moving away from. It defines a global var (var without a var keyword) called **exports** and attaches the module as a field within this var.

Listing 8-16. Code emitted from Listing 8-15 when targeting CommonJS

```
"use strict";
Object.defineProperty(exports, "__esModule", { value: true });
exports.createUrl = void 0;
const node_url_1 = require("node:url");
function createUrl(href) {
    return new node_url_1.URL(href);
}
exports.createUrl = createUrl;
```

Asynchronous Module Definition (AMD)

Created in 2011 as CommonJS remained unsupported by browsers as non-canon to ECMAScript standard, AMD – via the module loader RequireJS – became a way to simulate modules in browser JavaScript, largely deprecated nowadays. It uses a **define** function within RequireJS to manage loading a closure, which in turn (like CommonJS) adds the module to a global **exports** var.

Listing 8-17. Code emitted from Listing 8-15 when targeting AMD

```
define(["require", "exports", "node:url"],
    function (require, exports, node_url_1) {
    "use strict";
    Object.defineProperty(exports, "__esModule", { value:
    true });
    exports.createUrl = void 0;
    function createUrl(href) {
        return new node_url_1.URL(href);
    }
    exports.createUrl = createUrl;
});
```

Universal Module Definition (UMD)

Created later in 2011 as a way to host both CommonJS *and* AMD module conventions in a single JavaScript file, but not widely adopted by the industry as there was no clear market leader for a module loader for this more verbose practice.

Listing 8-18. Code emitted from Listing 8-15 when targeting UMD

```
(function (factory) {
    if (typeof module === "object" && typeof module.exports ===
    "object") {
        var v = factory(require, exports);
        if (v !== undefined) module.exports = v;
    }
    else if (typeof define === "function" && define.amd) {
        define(["require", "exports", "node:url"], factory);
    }
})(function (require, exports) {
```

```
    "use strict";
    Object.defineProperty(exports, "__esModule", { value:
    true });
    exports.createUrl = void 0;
    const node_url_1 = require("node:url");
    function createUrl(href) {
        return new node_url_1.URL(href);
    }
    exports.createUrl = createUrl;
});
```

SystemJS

Not actually a module system but included here to avoid confusion when referencing tsconfig.json module options, SystemJS is actually a module loader that (like RequireJS) has a particular syntax and so required a specific module output format – and like RequireJS, it used a named function to manage asynchronous load and the modules, although it used a return value rather than a global var. This, as well as AMD and UMD, is now largely deprecated by the JavaScript community in favor of the ESM native module format.

Listing 8-19. Code emitted from Listing 8-15 when targeting SystemJS

```
System.register(["node:url"], function (exports_1, context_1) {
    "use strict";
    var node_url_1;
    var __moduleName = context_1 && context_1.id;
    function createUrl(href) {
        return new node_url_1.URL(href);
    }
```

```
    exports_1("createUrl", createUrl);
    return {
        setters: [
            function (node_url_1_1) {
                node_url_1 = node_url_1_1;
            }
        ],
        execute: function () {
        }
    };
});
```

ESM

ES modules, finally standardized in 2015, are the native implementation of modules. As TypeScript follows ECMAScript, the syntax for this is essentially identical (without the type notations) to what you will already be familiar with in TypeScript.

Listing 8-20. Code emitted from Listing 8-15 when targeting ESM

```
import { URL } from 'node:url';
export function createUrl(href) {
    return new URL(href);
}
```

Exports and Imports

By changing your tsconfig.json target, you can write code in ESM format and emit output in any of the aforementioned module formats. So let's cover this ESM format now and explore how to use it.

The ESM file format is defined by the use of the **import** and **export** keywords. Any file that does *not* either import or export a value or type is inferred to be a classic JavaScript file, and the values and types therein are added to the global scope. This means they are available in all files without additional import.

Once you include either an **import** or **export**, the game changes. Your file is processed instead as an ESM module, and any values and types therein are only available to other values and types within the same file. To use them in other files (modules), you need to first **export** them from your file and then **import** them into the desired consuming module.

To export a value or type, just prefix the value or type with the **export** keyword:

Listing 8-21. Exporting values and types from a module

```
// Export a constant or variable:
export const greeting = 'Hello world!'

// Export a function:
export function greet(name: string) {
    return `Hello ${name}!`;
}

// Export an interface:
export interface Person {
    firstName: string
    lastName: string
}

// Export a type alias:
export type PersonKey = keyof Person;
```

279

You can also export them using an export statement:

Listing 8-22. Exporting values and types from a module using a single statement

```
const greeting = 'Hello world!'
interface Person {
    firstName: string
    lastName: string
}
export { greeting, Person };
```

To make compilation simpler (so that TypeScript doesn't need to work out which imports/exports to exclude during transpilation), you can also mark the exports with an optional **type** keyword hint to indicate they are type exports:

Listing 8-23. Using type hints on exports to help the compiler

```
export { greet, type Person };
```

Importing is similar, although you have two options: importing synchronously during module load and importing asynchronously and conditionally during runtime.

Importing synchronously during module load is the most common practice and has a similar syntax to exporting:

Listing 8-24. Importing values and types from a module

```
import { greet, Person } from './module.js';

console.log(greet('Dave'));  // Outputs 'Hello Dave!'
```

Like when exporting, you can optionally add the **type** keyword as an optimization hint to the TypeScript compiler to help save it a few steps during compilation when working out whether to exclude imports from emitted code:

Listing 8-25. Using type hints on imports to help the compiler

```
import { greet, type Person } from './module.js';
```

Note that the module file name in TypeScript needs to be suffixed with the file extension of the emitted file, not the source file. The reason for this is to keep the highest parity with the final code, and the **allowImportingTsExtensions** tsconfig option only works when no code will be emitted for this very reason.

You can also alias imports using the **as** keyword as well as re-export imports, as shown in the following code:

Listing 8-26. Renaming imports using the as keyword

```
import { greet as renderGreeting } from './module.js';
// Use alias
console.log(renderGreeting('Dave'));

import * as MyModule from './module.js';   // Import everything
                                           // from a module
console.log(MyModule.greet('Dave'));

export { type Person } from './module.js'; // Re-export the
                                           // type or value
```

The imports covered so far are performed when the module is loaded. But if instead you want to *conditionally* import a module based on runtime logic, you can also import it via an inline import:

Listing 8-27. ESM supports conditional (runtime) asynchronous imports, as well as the normal bundle-time ones.

```
function async createGreetingAsync(name: string) {
    let greeting = 'Hello'
    if (features.translationEnabled) {
        const translator =
            await import('./hugeTranslatorModule.js');
        greeting = translator(greeting);
    }
    return `${greeting} ${name}`;
}
```

The conditional import approach allows you to exclude some optional pieces of your code from your main bundle and deliver these in increments after your app is mainly up and running, to provide a faster, smoother, experience for the user.

How TypeScript Resolves Modules

Module "resolution" means the process TypeScript uses to find the file that an **import** statement refers to. TypeScript can be set to resolve in either "Classic" or "Node" mode. Classic mode is only included for compatibility with early versions of TypeScript and can be ignored; Node module resolution mode instead copies the resolution process that Node.js (and other compatible runtimes) uses and is now TypeScript's default module resolution mode.

This "Node" module resolution mode works as shown in Figure 8-1.

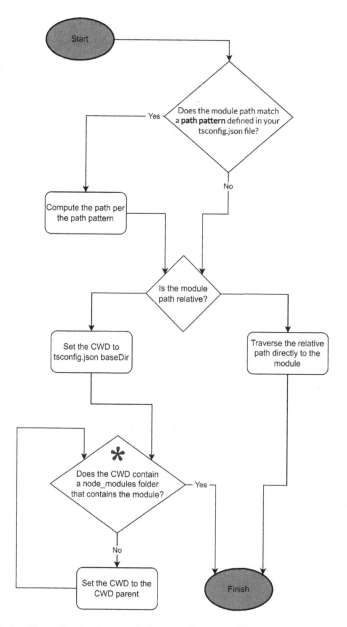

Figure 8-1. *TypeScript's module resolution algorithm*

When TypeScript evaluates the step marked with an asterisk (*) in the preceding Node.js algorithm, there are a few substeps that are worth detailing. These begin by determining whether the module path requested is a path to a module folder only (e.g., "react"), or to a specific file within a module (e.g., "zod/lib/helpers/util.js").

If the path is to a module folder, the algorithm loads the package.json within that folder and traverses to the entrypoint specified in the package. json's "main" entry and the type definitions specified in its "types" entry. If these entries do not exist, then it'll check some default file names instead. If the path is to a specific module file, the algorithm instead tries to jump directly to that file.

However, in both the case of checking default file names *and* if jumping directly to a specific module file, if the file name in question has no extension specified, then lastly the algorithm will try the following possible extensions for this: .ts, .mts, .cts, .tsx, .mtsx, .ctsx, .d.ts, .js, .mjs, .mjsx, .cjs, and .cjsx.

As you can see from the aforementioned, there are quite a few options attempted when trying to resolve modules. Adding main/types to your package.json will help shortcut this, but let's review a hardest-possible resolution within a monorepo to illustrate the algorithm in action:

Listing 8-28. Example steps when resolving a module

```
import { someValue } from 'my-custom-package';
```

Resolving:
> 'my-custom-package' is not a relative module path ✗
> 'my-custom-package' is not in path patterns in
  tsconfig.json ✗
> **'/src/packages/myPackage/node_modules' exists ✓**
> '/src/packages/myPackage/node_modules/my-custom-package'
  does not exist ✗
> '/src/packages/node_modules' does not exist ✗

> '/src/node_modules' does not exist ✗
> **'/node_modules' exists** ✓
> **'/node_modules/my-custom-package' exists** ✓
> **'/node_modules/my-custom-package/package.json' exists** ✓
> my-custom-package package.json does not contain a main entry ✗
> '/node_modules/my-custom-package/index.ts' does not exist ✗
> '/node_modules/my-custom-package/index.mts' does not exist ✗
> '/node_modules/my-custom-package/index.cts' does not exist ✗
> '/node_modules/my-custom-package/index.tsx' does not exist ✗
> '/node_modules/my-custom-package/index.mtsx' does not exist ✗
> '/node_modules/my-custom-package/index.ctsx' does not exist ✗
> '/node_modules/my-custom-package/index.js' does not exist ✗
> '/node_modules/my-custom-package/index.mjs' does not exist ✗
> **'/node_modules/my-custom-package/index.cjs' exists** ✓
> **Resolved 'my-custom-package'='/node_modules/my-custom-package/index.cjs'** ✓

To debug your own imports, TypeScript includes a helpful **traceResolution** CLI parameter and tsconfig.json setting. Setting this to true will log to your STDOUT the results of its module resolution for every import in your project.

Listing 8-29. Command-line parameters to output module resolution steps

```
npx tsc --noEmit --traceResolution
```

Summary

In this chapter, you learned how the key aspects of TypeScript's build process work and how you can configure them to your advantage. We explored configuration and extending it with linting, as well as JSX syntax and its relation to standard JavaScript/TypeScript; and we dug deep into module formats and how imports, exports, and module resolution work.

To recap, we started off with TypeScript's powerful build configurations and the core configuration for this: the **tsconfig.json** file. We started by exploring compiler options, which allow you to control how TypeScript compiles your code. In this section, I presented a recommended suite of settings that were tailored for modern development and with a focus on ensuring code quality and maintainability.

We then also covered how to improve even further on the static test provided by TypeScript by using a complementary suite of quality-focused ESLint rules. We discussed the rules I propose as a sensible default for all projects and the reasoning behind each. These rules were unopinionated in that they were focused on error prevention rather than stylistic assertions, as it is best to decide stylistic rules in the context of your team's own preferences. Using this recommended lint ruleset provides additional safety checks that minimize potential issues.

Next we explored the JSX/TSX syntax and discovered how it is just syntactic sugar atop our existing JavaScript runtime. As such, we explored how we can use the TypeScript type-safety techniques learned in this book and apply them to JSX/TSX files too. This means you can use advanced types, such as computed return values, union type props, intersections, and more in your React/TSX code to provide a high degree of type safety as well as improve the autocomplete suggestions in your IDE.

Finally, we dived into modules – what they were, their formats, and how TypeScript works with them. Understanding the ESM format, imports, exports, and module resolution strategies enables you to organize your code effectively and utilize TypeScript's module system to its fullest potential. With this understanding, you are now equipped to make informed decisions about code organization, dependencies, and post-compilation tasks such as bundling and chunking.

With the knowledge gained in this chapter, you are well equipped to manage your TypeScript projects efficiently. As you progress in your TypeScript journey, the skills acquired in this chapter will serve as a solid foundation for setting up and configuring more complex projects in the way that you and your team need.

CHAPTER 9

Wrap Up

Congratulations, dear reader! By reaching this point, you will have gained full mastery of this powerful tooling that will revolutionize your coding journey. You are now equipped with the insights and expertise needed to craft scalable and maintainable projects, even in the most complex scenarios.

Your journey through this book has covered a wide landscape. We have explored the roots of TypeScript and the imperative needs it fulfills within the evolving JavaScript community. We have embraced the core concepts of structural typing and how this interacts with a functional but dynamic approach to coding. We have delved into advanced concepts, such as advanced type inference, type widening and narrowing, type assertions, and parameterized types. We have covered computed types, such as unions, intersections, generics, and mapped and recursive types. And we have seen how all these can be used together to create the built-in utility types, improvements on them, and even more advanced types that take advantage of the power of structural and dynamic typing.

Beyond types, you've also become an expert now in setting up optimal TypeScript projects. You understand the configuration options in depth, as well as how to extend these using additional rules from ESLint. We have also looked at a number of the most cutting-edge TypeScript packages available and explored how some of them can even further your journey.

© Ben Beattie-Hood 2023
B. Beattie-Hood, *Modern TypeScript*, https://doi.org/10.1007/978-1-4842-9723-0_9

Now, as you stand on what is now a mountaintop of expertise, take a moment now to enjoy your accomplishments. You are now a wizard of TypeScript. Your newfound understanding empowers you to guide others on this transformative journey, reducing errors and enabling your team to embark on a high-velocity coding adventure.

But remember, the learning never truly ends. Embrace the curiosity that fuels your passion for coding and continue to explore the ever-evolving world of TypeScript. As you share your knowledge and experiences with others, you'll inspire a community of developers to unlock the full potential of TypeScript and create a brighter future for software development.

So fellow coder, let the adventure continue! Armed with the knowledge and wisdom you've gained, embrace the challenges that lie ahead and create masterpieces that help shape the digital landscape for others to come. Happy coding!

Index

A

Abstract classes and
    methods, 88, 98
abstract keyword, 88
Access modifiers, 81, 82,
    84, 85, 87
Anonymous types, 104, 105, 215
Any type, 67, 68, 262
Arrays, 28, 33–37, 142,
    156, 175, 180
  function values, 194
  of globs, 246
  JsonOf, 193
  optional fields, 202
  tuple, 197
as keyword, 50–52, 171, 281
Assertion
  compiletime, 49–52, 55, 78,
    182, 209
  runtime, 24, 49, 59–64,
    67, 127
Assignments, 260
Async, 37, 39, 78, 258
Asynchronous Module Definition
  (AMD), 4, 275, 276
Auto-narrowing, 45–48
await, 37, 258

B

Babel, 246, 274
Browserlist, 240
Bun tool, 15

C

Caching types, 14, 160, 214,
  221–222, 232
Chromium-based browser, 230
Civet, 15, 16, 209
Classes
  access modifiers, 82
  constructors, 82
  ECMAScript, 82
  fields, 83–86
  functional programming
    techniques, 81
  getters and setters, 86
  implements keyword, 89–92
  inheritance, 87–89
  methods, 87
  object-oriented programming, 81
  structuring code, 81
  warning
    not types, 93–95
    scope bleed problem, 95–98

© Ben Beattie-Hood 2023
B. Beattie-Hood, *Modern TypeScript*, https://doi.org/10.1007/978-1-4842-9723-0

Printed in the United States
by Baker & Taylor Publisher Services